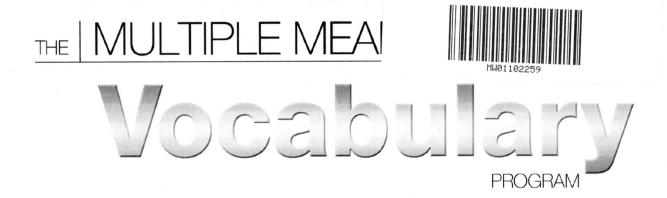

THE MULTIPLE MEANING Vocabulary PROGRAM

Student Lesson Book
Level II

J. Ron Nelson, Ph.D.
&
Nancy Marchand-Martella, Ph.D.

SOPRIS WEST EDUCATIONAL SERVICES
A CAMBIUM LEARNING COMPANY

BOSTON, MA • NEW YORK, NY • LONGMONT, CO

Published and Distributed by

SOPRIS
WEST
EDUCATIONAL SERVICES

4093 Specialty Place • Longmont, Colorado 80504
(303) 651-2829 • www.sopriswest.com

267STU2/2-05/BAN

CONTENTS

Apart

Pre-Lesson Activity—Meanings of Related Words

1 One meaning of **apart** includes the following related words.

a. **Away from** means <u>some distance from one another</u>. For example, "Bess said that her grandmother lived 20 miles **away from** from her."
Write a sentence using **away from**.

_____

_____

b. **Separated from** means that there is <u>some distance from one another</u> or between things. For example, "The two farms were **separated from** one another by 50 miles."
Write a sentence using **separated from**.

_____

_____

c. **Spread** can mean having <u>some distance from one another</u> or between things. For example, "She was standing there with her feet **spread**."
Write a sentence using **spread**.

_____

_____

2 A second meaning of **apart** includes the following related words.

a. **Into pieces** means something <u>breaks into parts</u>. For example, "Kim broke the glass bowl **into pieces** when she dropped it on the brick patio."
Write a sentence using **into pieces**.

_____

_____

b. **To shreds** means something is torn into pieces or <u>breaks into parts</u>. For example, "Jason tore the old newspaper **to shreds** to help start the campfire."
Write a sentence using **to shreds**.

_____

_____

c. **Asunder** means <u>broken into parts</u>. For example, "The war tore the country **asunder**."
Write a sentence using **asunder**.

_____

_____

3 A third meaning of **apart** includes the following related words.

   a. **Except** means an <u>exception to a general statement</u>. For example, "Bill ate all of his meal **except** for his brussel sprouts."

      Write a sentence using **except**.

      _____

      _____

   b. **Excluding** means that an <u>exception to a general statement</u> is made. For example, "Betina weeded the garden, **excluding** the row of corn."

      Write a sentence using **excluding**.

      _____

      _____

   c. **Bar** can mean an <u>exception to a general statement</u>. For example, "Shelby washed all the windows she could reach **bar** the one that required a ladder."

      Write a sentence using **bar**.

      _____

      _____

4 A fourth meaning of **apart** includes the following related words.

   a. **Alone** can mean <u>by oneself</u>. For example, "The new girl in the neighborhood rode her bike **alone** from the other children."

      Write a sentence using **alone**.

      _____

      _____

   b. **Cut off** means <u>by oneself</u> and removed from others. For example, "Their campsite was **cut off** from the other campsites because they wanted their privacy."

      Write a sentence using **cut off**.

      _____

      _____

   c. **Isolated** can mean <u>by oneself</u>. For example, "Mr. Moore was new to the club and sat **isolated** from the other men."

      Write a sentence using **isolated**.

      _____

      _____

Word Meaning in Context

Apart began in the Latin language as a word meaning "at or to the side."
Later, in the English language, this meaning expanded to include four
current meanings:

- ❏ **some distance from one another**
- ❏ **break into parts**
- ❏ **exception to a general statement**
- ❏ **by oneself**

1. The shy boy sat **apart** from the other children at the party.

Which of the meanings of **apart** is this?_____

_____

2. Jayla and her friend, Tessa, lived 50 miles **apart**.

Which of the meanings of **apart** is this?_____

_____

3. Uncle Jake said, "If you drop the clock on floor it will fall **apart**."

Which of the meanings of **apart** is this?_____

_____

4. She had no money **apart** from the dollar bill her father gave her.

Which of the meanings of **apart** is this?_____

_____

Word Meaning Map   The teacher will give you the **Apart** worksheet.

Complete Each Definition

1. **Apart** can mean some _____
from one another.

2. **Apart** can also mean to _____
something into parts.

3. **Apart** from can also mean an _____
to a general statement.

4. **Apart** can also mean by _____.

Understanding Check

Circle whether **apart** is used as you would expect.

1. Thomas and his friend Kyle sold candy for three weeks. The funds from the candy sales were set **apart** from the rest of the budget for the annual campout.

   Expect   Not Expect

2. Jessica and Jennifer were twins. They were the same in every way. It was easy to tell them **apart** from one another.

   Expect   Not Expect

3. John was sad because his rocket ship fell **apart**.

   Expect   Not Expect

4. Kevin and his family lived in a big house in the country. The railings on the back porch were three feet **apart**.

   Expect   Not Expect

5. Terrence knew the new car was well made and built to last for years because it fell **apart** on the highway.

   Expect   Not Expect

6. Shawn believed the reason he could not visit his grandmother was because they lived too far **apart**. They lived next door to one another.

   Expect   Not Expect

7. Deb had not been jogging in ages and was out of shape. She jogged **apart** from the other runners who had been jogging for years.

   Expect   Not Expect

8. Rainey was very friendly and loved interacting with people. She sat **apart** from her friends at the ice cream social.

   Expect   Not Expect

Create Stories

On a sheet of paper, write a short story or scenario for each of the four meanings of **apart**.

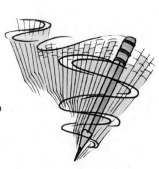

Pre-Lesson Activity—Meanings of Related Words

1 One meaning of **argue** includes the following related words.

   a. To **bicker** with someone means that you <u>disagree</u> with what he has to say. For example, "Jeff began to **bicker** with his brother over who would ride the new bicycle."

      Write a sentence using **bicker**.

      _____

      _____

   b. To **quarrel** with someone is to <u>disagree</u> with her in an angry manner. For example, "Mary was upset with Kate when she did not share the pizza so she began to **quarrel** with her."

      Write a sentence using **quarrel**.

      _____

      _____

   c. When people **squabble** about something, they <u>disagree</u> about something unimportant. For example, "The children started to **squabble** over who could play on the swingset."

      Write a sentence using **squabble**.

      _____

      _____

2 A second meaning of **argue** includes the following related words.

   a. To **make a case** for something is to <u>give reasons why</u> you support it or are against it. For example, "Our school was asked to **make a case** for the band equipment, given the limited school budget."

      Write a sentence using **make a case**.

      _____

      _____

b. If you **contend** that something is true, you <u>give reasons why</u> you think it is. For example, "Brianna started to **contend** that missing the school meeting was important."

Write a sentence using **contend**.

_____

_____

c. If you **maintain** something, you state your opinion or <u>give reasons why</u> you think as you do. For example, "Brett tried to **maintain** his innocence by telling everyone that he was just borrowing the radio rather than stealing it."

Write a sentence using **maintain**.

_____

_____

3 A third meaning of **argue** includes the following related words.

a. **Demonstrate** can mean to <u>show that something is the case</u>. For example, "Mary's paintings **demonstrate** her artistic talents."

Write a sentence using **demonstrate**.

_____

_____

b. **Indicate** means to <u>show that something is the case</u>. For example, "Avril's flower gardens **indicate** her "green thumb," or how good she is at gardening.

Write a sentence using **indicate**.

_____

_____

c. **Display** can mean to <u>show that something is the case</u>. For example, "The cheesecakes that John made **display** his excellent skills in baking."

Write a sentence using **display**.

_____

_____

Word Meaning in Context

Argue began in the Old French language as a word meaning "by oneself." Later, in the English language, this meaning changed to include three current meanings:

- ❏ **disagree**
- ❏ **give reasons why**
- ❏ **show that something is the case**

1. Clay tried to **argue** for why his bike was the best in the neighborhood.

Which of the meanings of **argue** is this? _____

_____

2. Craig likes to refinish furniture. The tables he completed **argue** how well he is at fixing old furniture.

Which of the meanings of **argue** is this? _____

_____

3. Seth and his sister Becky began to **argue** over who was going to get to sit in the front seat of the car on the way home from the grocery store.

Which of the meanings of **argue** is this? _____

_____

Word Meaning Map   The teacher will give you the **Argue** worksheet.

Complete Each Definition

1. **Argue** can mean to _____ with someone about something.

2. **Argue** can also mean to give _____ why you believe as you do.

3. **Argue** can also mean to show that something is the _____.

The Multiple Meaning Vocabulary Program   TARGET WORD—**Argue** | **7**

Understanding Check

Circle whether **argue** is used as you would expect.

1. Samantha enjoyed school, especially speech class. In this class she had to **argue** why she believed we needed to do things for the school, such as recycle cans and bottles.

   Expect   Not Expect

2. Tracy and Vickie were the best of friends and always thought the same way. They always seemed to **argue** during study hall.

   Expect   Not Expect

3. Rosa was excellent at decorating her home. The living room in particular would **argue** for her skills in home decorating.

   Expect   Not Expect

4. Nan hired people to paint her house because she was not good at painting. Her painting skills would **argue** her talent in painting homes for others.

   Expect   Not Expect

5. Austin did not like to do the dishes. Austin and his sister Amy tended to **argue** about whose turn it was to do the dishes after supper.

   Expect   Not Expect

6. Everyone believed Martin was right when he skipped the meeting to help his grandmother. He then had to **argue** why he missed the meeting.

   Expect   Not Expect

Create Stories

On a sheet of paper, write a short story or scenario for each of the three meanings of **argue**.

Arrange

Pre-Lesson Activity—Meanings of Related Words

1 One meaning of **arrange** includes the following related words.

a. When you **set up** something, you <u>make plans</u> concerning it. For example, "Ramon decided to **set up** a party for his best friend."

Write a sentence using **set up**.

_____

_____

b. To **coordinate** something means that you <u>make plans</u> with regard to it. For example, "Terry had to **coordinate** the first soccer meeting of the season to ensure that all those who wanted to play soccer would come."

Write a sentence using **coordinate**.

_____

_____

c. When we **organize** something, we <u>make plans</u> concerning it. For example, "Jeremy was asked to **organize** the going-away party for Mr. Lynch."

Write a sentence using **organize**.

_____

_____

2 A second meaning of **arrange** includes the following related words.

a. When we **place** something we <u>put it in a particular way</u> or order. For example, "Please **place** the knives next to the forks in the silverware tray."

Write a sentence using **place**.

_____

_____

b. To **assemble** things means that they are <u>put in a particular order or way</u>. For example, "Leo was told to **assemble** the room by placing four chairs at every table."

Write a sentence using **assemble**.

_____

_____

c. When you **position** something, you <u>put it in a particular way</u> or put it in a certain place. For example, "Mara had to **position** pillows around her leg to help ease the pain after her knee surgery."

Write a sentence using **position**.

_____

_____

3 A third meaning of **arrange** includes the following related words.

a. **Orchestrate** can mean to <u>change voices or instruments in an original piece of music</u>. For example, "The musician had to **orchestrate** the symphony so it could be performed without a piano by a marching band."

Write a sentence using **orchestrate**.

_____

_____

b. **Adapt** can mean to add, delete, or <u>change voices or instruments in an original piece of music</u>. For example, "The musician had to **adapt** the song to include trumpets since no one in the band played trombone, as called for in the original music."

Write a sentence using **adapt**.

_____

_____

c. **Score** can mean to <u>change voices or instruments in an original piece of music</u>. For example, "In her music class, she learned how to **score** a piece of music."

Write a sentence using **score**.

_____

_____

Word Meaning in Context

Arrange began in the Old French language as a word meaning "set in a row." Later, in the English language, this meaning changed to its three current meanings:

- ❏ **make plans**
- ❏ **put in a particular way**
- ❏ **change voices or instruments in an original piece of music**

1. The musician had to **arrange** the music so Havana, who played the harp, could be included in the concert.

Which of the meanings of **arrange** is this? _____

_____

2. Sam needed to **arrange** a visit to the dentist to get his teeth cleaned.

Which of the meanings of **arrange** is this? _____

_____

3. Ms. Kristen asked us to **arrange** the chairs in the room so that everyone could see the blackboard.

Which of the meanings of **arrange** is this? _____

_____

Word Meaning Map   The teacher will give you the **Arrange** worksheet.

Complete Each Definition

1. **Arrange** can mean to make _____.

2. **Arrange** can also mean to put in a _____

_____ way.

3. **Arrange** can also mean to change voices or instruments in an _____

_____ piece of music.

✔ Understanding Check

Circle whether **arrange** is used as you would expect.

1. Theodora needed to **arrange** her schedule so that she could get her hair cut before she interviewed for a new job.

    Expect   Not Expect

2. Jessie cut roses and daisies from her flower garden. She then had to **arrange** them in a vase.

    Expect   Not Expect

3. Kiera had to **arrange** the notebooks from smallest to largest. The notebooks were not placed in any particular order by Kiera.

    Expect   Not Expect

4. Fred was able to **arrange** his class schedule. Therefore, he was not sure what he would take this school year.

    Expect   Not Expect

5. No changes were needed in the music the symphony would play. Therefore, the musicians needed to **arrange** the original music.

    Expect   Not Expect

6. Tristan had to **arrange** the music to allow flutes and piccolos to be included. Now everyone could participate in the concert.

    Expect   Not Expect

Create Stories

On a sheet of paper, write a short story or scenario for each of the three meanings of **arrange**.

Attention

Pre-Lesson Activity—Meanings of Related Words

1 One meaning of **attention** includes the following related words.

   a. **Concentration** can mean to hold one's <u>focus on something for a period of time</u>. For example, "Bobbie needed his full **concentration** to complete the tough math story problems."

   Write a sentence using **concentration**.

_____

_____

   b. **Thought** can mean to hold one's <u>focus on something for some period of time</u>. For example, "Jean needs to give full **thought** to her research paper on planets if she is to do well."

   Write a sentence using **thought**.

_____

_____

   c. **Diligence** means to keep one's <u>focus on something for a period of time</u>. For example, "Her **diligence** in searching for her long-lost father paid off when she finally located him in a nearby town."

   Write a sentence using **diligence**.

_____

_____

2 A second meaning of **attention** includes the following related words.

   a. **Regard** can mean to <u>notice</u> something or others. For example, "Elden seemed to give no **regard** to the boys who were yelling at him."

   Write a sentence using **regard**.

_____

_____

b. **Heed** can mean to <u>notice</u> something. For example, "He paid no **heed** to the doctor's advice to stay in bed for a few days and went to the movie."

Write a sentence using **heed**.

_____

_____

c. **Concern** can mean to <u>notice</u> something. For example, "As she drove past at a high speed, Lucy showed little **concern** for the woman standing on the street waving at her to slow down."

Write a sentence using **concern**.

_____

_____

3 A third meaning of **attention** has no related words.

a. When **attention** is used in this way, it means <u>a position assumed by a soldier</u> with heels together, body straight, arms to the sides, and eyes to the front. For example, "The soldier stood at **attention** during the ceremony."

Write a sentence using **attention**.

_____

_____

Word Meaning in Context

Attention began in the Latin language as a word meaning "to heed."
Later, in the English language, this meaning expanded to its three
current meanings:

- ❏ **focus on something for a period of time**
- ❏ **notice**
- ❏ **position assumed by a soldier**

1. When the flag was raised above the crowd, the soldiers stood at **attention**.

Which of the meanings of **attention** is this?_____

_____

2. The teacher asked the students to give their full **attention** while they are taking the test.

Which of the meanings of **attention** is this?_____

_____

3. Nobody paid any **attention** to the thunderstorm warning.

Which of the meanings of **attention** is this?_____

_____

Word Meaning Map   The teacher will give you the **Attention** worksheet.

Complete Each Definition

1. **Attention** can mean to _____ something.

2. **Attention** can also mean a position assumed by a _____

_____.

3. **Attention** can also mean to _____ on something
for a period of time.

Understanding Check

Circle whether **attention** is used as you would expect.

1. The soldier was standing with heels together, body straight, arms to the sides, and eyes to the front. He was not standing at **attention**.

   Expect   Not Expect

2. We visited Washington, DC. We saw many soldiers standing at **attention** at the gate in front of the White House.

   Expect   Not Expect

3. Blake's full **attention** was on cleaning the garage before his parents came home. He began daydreaming about his baseball game that night while he sat down on a box in the garage.

   Expect   Not Expect

4. Mrs. Mavin asked all the students to try their best during the spelling quiz. Sarah, a student in Mrs. Mavin's class, turned her **attention** to the quiz rather than on writing in her journal.

   Expect   Not Expect

5. Shelly paid no **attention** to the sign in the hallway that read, "Slippery when wet." She stopped, turned around, and went down another hallway.

   Expect   Not Expect

6. The flashing lights caught Sherman's **attention**. He quickly looked in their direction.

   Expect   Not Expect

Create Stories

On a sheet of paper, write a short story or scenario for each of the three meanings of **attention**.

Bargain

Pre-Lesson Activity—Meanings of Related Words

1 One meaning of **bargain** includes the following related words.

   a. To **haggle** is to <u>discuss</u> or argue about what you will pay for something. For example, "Mrs. Jamison liked to **haggle** over the prices of items at garage sales."

   Write a sentence using **haggle**.

   _____

   _____

   b. To **negotiate** is to <u>discuss</u> a situation with someone to solve a problem. For example, "George had to **negotiate** with his father to ride his friend's motorcycle."

   Write a sentence using **negotiate**.

   _____

   _____

   c. When you **dicker** with others, you <u>discuss</u> or argue about what you will pay for something. For example, "After seeing the high price of the stereo, Jay began to **dicker** with the salesman so he could get it for a lower price."

   Write a sentence using **dicker**.

   _____

   _____

2 A second meaning of **bargain** includes the following related words.

   a. To get something at a "**steal**" means that you paid far less than the usual cost for the item or got a <u>good deal</u>. For example, "Marian said that she got the new car for a '**steal**' because she paid $5,000 less than the sticker price."

   Write a sentence using "**steal**."

   _____

   _____

b. A **markdown** means that something is priced at a lower than normal price or is considered a <u>good deal</u>. For example, "Eric got a **markdown** on the new mountain bike; he paid $200 less than the asking price and also got a free helmet."

Write a sentence using a **markdown**.

_____

_____

c. A **discount** is a <u>good deal</u> because the price is lower than usual. For example, "We got the new pool at a **discount**, paying only $100 for it."

Write a sentence using **discount**.

_____

_____

3 A third meaning of **bargain** includes the following related words.

a. A **contract** is a formal <u>agreement</u> between two or more persons or parties. For example, "Paying for your dentist bill was not part of our **contract**."

Write a sentence using **contract**.

_____

_____

b. A **pact** is a formal <u>agreement</u> between two or more persons or parties. For example, "Jill made a **pact** with her sister to watch her nieces in exchange for living at her sister's house in the summer."

Write a sentence using **pact**.

_____

_____

c. A **promise** is an <u>agreement</u> that you will definitely do something. For example, "Shelby made a **promise** to help her neighbors move into their new home if they agreed to plow the snow in her driveway in the winter."

Write a sentence using **promise**.

_____

_____

Word Meaning in Context

Bargain began in the Old French language as a word meaning "haggle."
Later, in the English language, this meaning expanded to include three
current meanings:

- ❑ **discuss what to do or to pay**
- ❑ **good deal**
- ❑ **agreement**

1. The **bargain** Erica and her parents agreed to was that she needed to earn enough money to buy the bike.

Which of the meanings of **bargain** is this? _____

_____

2. Bobbie attempted to **bargain** with her sister about who would do the dishes after supper.

Which of the meanings of **bargain** is this? _____

_____

3. Max got a real **bargain** on his new trumpet at the music store.

Which of the meanings of **bargain** is this? _____

_____

Word Meaning Map   The teacher will give you the **Bargain** worksheet.

Complete Each Definition

1. **Bargain** can mean that you got a good _____
because you bought something for less than the normal price.

2. **Bargain** can also mean an _____ between two or more
people describing what each of them will do.

3. **Bargain** can also mean to _____ what to do or to pay
for something.

Understanding Check

Circle whether **bargain** is used as you would expect.

1. Hailey and Gabriel loved to play together at recess. They attempted to **bargain** with their teacher to give them extra recess time.

   Expect   Not Expect

2. Bailey paid more for his car than it was worth. The car was a real **bargain**.

   Expect   Not Expect

3. Cameron's mother finally reached a **bargain** with the antique dealer over how much she would pay for the brown rocking chair.

   Expect   Not Expect

4. Rafael got a great **bargain** on a pair of in-line skates at the mall. He paid ten dollars less than his friend did for the same skates.

   Expect   Not Expect

5. Ronda loved to **bargain** with others over prices. When she went to the yard sale, she paid full price for everything.

   Expect   Not Expect

6. Rita and Mr. Jones struck a **bargain** on who would weed the garden and mow the lawn. Rita left Mr. Jones' house saying that they could not agree on any of the outside work.

   Expect   Not Expect

Create Stories

On a sheet of paper, write a short story or scenario for each of the three meanings of **bargain**.

TARGET WORD |

Pre-Lesson Activity—Meanings of Related Words

1 One meaning of **boil** includes the following related words.

a. **Cook** can mean to <u>heat something in water or another liquid</u>. For example, "Manley had to **cook** the carrots in water to soften them."

Write a sentence using **cook**.

_____

_____

b. **Stew** can mean to <u>heat something in water or another liquid</u> slowly over time. For example, "Marlee helped her mother **stew** the soup mixture on the stove."

Write a sentence using **stew**.

_____

_____

c. **Brew** can mean to <u>heat something in water or another liquid</u>, such as coffee grounds or tea leaves. For example, "Please **brew** some coffee for my grandmother."

Write a sentence using **brew**.

_____

_____

2 A second meaning of **boil** includes the following related words.

a. **Mad** can mean to be <u>angry</u> at someone or something. For example, "Seeing her friends go out rather than helping her on the class project made Melissa **mad**."

Write a sentence using **mad**.

_____

_____

b. **Fume** can mean to be very <u>angry</u> at someone or something. For example, "When Jason left without helping his father mow the lawn, his father began to **fume**."

Write a sentence using **fume**.

_____

_____

c. **Seethe** can mean to be very <u>angry</u> about something but not able to show your feelings about it. For example, "When the repairman did not show up on time, Mr. Johanson began to **seethe** with anger."

Write a sentence using **seethe**.

_____

_____

3 A third meaning of **boil** includes the following related words.

a. An **abscess** can be a red-looking <u>blister-like area on the skin</u>. For example, "The **abscess** on Ed's finger was so painful that he needed to go to the health clinic."

Write a sentence using **abscess**.

_____

_____

b. A **sore** can be a <u>blister-like area on the skin</u>. For example, "Shelby had a **sore** on her elbow that needed to be examined by a doctor."

Write a sentence using **sore**.

_____

_____

c. A **lesion** is a <u>blister-like area on the skin</u> that is painful. For example, "Isabelle's finger had a painful **lesion** on it that prevented her from going into the pool to swim."

Write a sentence using **lesion**.

_____

_____

Word Meaning in Context

Boil began in the Latin language as a word meaning "bubble." Later, in the English language, this meaning expanded to include three current meanings:

❑ **heat something in water or another liquid**

❑ **angry**

❑ **blister-like area on the skin**

1. The **boil** on Victor's leg hurt.

Which of the meanings of **boil** is this? _____

_____

2. You must **boil** the broth to make a cup of soup.

Which of the meanings of **boil** is this? _____

_____

3. The mere idea of having to do extra chores made Teresa **boil**.

Which of the meanings of **boil** is this? _____

_____

Word Meaning Map

The teacher will give you the **Boil** worksheet.

Complete Each Definition

1. **Boil** can mean to _____ a liquid, such as water, to a high temperature causing it to bubble and produce steam.

2. **Boil** can also mean when someone becomes _____ over something or someone.

3. **Boil** can also mean a _____-like area on the skin.

Understanding Check

Circle whether **boil** is used as you would expect.

1. Niko took the bus downtown to the library every Saturday. Seeing people throw trash on the street made Niko **boil**.

   Expect   Not Expect

2. Alice loved cooked green beans. Alice had to **boil** water to cook the green beans.

   Expect   Not Expect

3. Toby and his family lived in the mountains. Toby loved it when it snowed. The snowstorm made him **boil**.

   Expect   Not Expect

4. Adam's teacher noticed him walking with a limp. Adam had to go to the doctor because of the painful **boil** on his leg.

   Expect   Not Expect

5. Mrs. Martinez said that ice-cold water should be used when making piecrusts. Sarah immediately started to **boil** some water.

   Expect   Not Expect

6. Jolene was the healthiest child in the family. She never got sick or had any infections. She had a **boil** on her arm.

   Expect   Not Expect

Create Stories

On a sheet of paper, write a short story or scenario for each of the three meanings of **boil**.

Pre-Lesson Activity—Meanings of Related Words

1 One meaning of **bore** includes the following related words.

a. **Tire** can mean to cause a person to be sleepy and <u>uninterested</u>. For example, "Listening to my parents talk about taxes and insurance really does **tire** me."

Write a sentence using **tire**.

_____

_____

b. **Dull person** can mean that someone is dull, boring, and <u>uninteresting</u>. For example, "The children said Mrs. Fielding was a **dull person** because she did not talk very much."

Write a sentence using **dull person**.

_____

_____

c. **Fatigue** can mean to be dull and <u>uninteresting</u>. For example, "The guest speaker really did **fatigue** me during his talk."

Write a sentence using **fatigue**.

_____

_____

2 A second meaning of **bore** includes the following related words.

a. **Drill** can mean to <u>make a hole</u> in or through something. For example, "My mother had to **drill** a hole in the table leg to put in a new screw to hold it in place."

Write a sentence using **drill**.

_____

_____

b. **Tunnel** can mean to <u>make a hole</u> or passage through or under something. For example, "The men had to **tunnel** into the cave wall to make a new passage."

Write a sentence using **tunnel**.

_____

_____

c. **Dig** can mean to <u>make a hole</u> or to break up or remove dirt or sand with a shovel. For example, "Dan had to **dig** a hole in the ground for his new flagpole."

Write a sentence using **dig**.

_____

_____

3 A third meaning of **bore** includes the following related words.

a. **Yielded** can mean when something has <u>produced</u> things, such as fruit or vegetables. For example, "The raspberry bush **yielded** large berries all summer long."

Write a sentence using **yielded**.

_____

_____

b. **Gave birth to** means that a female human or animal <u>produced</u> a child or offspring. For example, "My Aunt Sandy **gave birth to** a five-pound baby boy last weekend."

Write a sentence using **gave birth to**.

_____

_____

c. **Exhibited** can mean that something <u>produced</u> or showed certain characteristics or behaviors. For example, "Lela **exhibited** the same laugh and mannerisms as her father."

Write a sentence using **exhibited**.

_____

_____

4 A fourth meaning of **bore** includes the following related words.

a. **Shouldered** can mean that someone <u>supported the weight of something</u>. For example, "He **shouldered** most of the weight of the large box as he and his brother carried it upstairs."

Write a sentence using **shouldered**.

_____

_____

b. **Carried** can mean that you held or <u>supported the weight of an object</u> that you were moving. For example, "Chris **carried** the heavy plywood from the store to his pickup truck."

Write a sentence using **carried**.

_____

_____

c. **Lugged** can mean that someone <u>supported the weight of something</u> or carried it. For example, "Kit **lugged** the heavy suitcase from her car to the house."

Write a sentence using **lugged**.

_____

_____

Word Meaning in Context

Bore began in the Old German language as a word meaning "carry." Later, in the English language, this meaning expanded to include four current meanings:

- ❏ **uninterested or an uninteresting thing**
- ❏ **made a hole**
- ❏ **produced**
- ❏ **supported the weight of something**

1. Sabrina **bore** a heavy load of books in her backpack.

   Which of the meanings of **bore** is this?_____

   _____

2. Mr. Jones started to **bore** us with stories of when he was young. Cindy said the movie was a **bore** because she fell asleep during it.

   Which of the meanings of **bore** are these? _____

   _____

3. Randy helped Danielle **bore** a hole through a piece of wood with a power drill.

   Which of the meanings of **bore** is this?_____

   _____

4. The apple tree **bore** delicious fruit every fall. Anna **bore** a striking resemblance to her mother.

   Which of the meanings of **bore** are these? _____

   _____

Word Meaning Map   The teacher will give you the **Bore** worksheet.

Complete Each Definition

1. **Bore** can mean uninteresting or an _____ thing.

2. **Bore** can also mean when someone made a _____ in something.

3. **Bore** can also mean _____ , as in the yield of a fruit tree.

4. **Bore** can also mean supported the _____ of something.

 ## Understanding Check

Circle whether **bore** is used as you would expect.

1. The trader used his horse to haul things. His horse **bore** a heavy pack with saddlebags filled with furs.   Expect   Not Expect

2. A tree in Leah's backyard **bore** wonderful peaches each year. Leah and her mother loved to bake peach cobbler with the peaches they picked.   Expect   Not Expect

3. Kristin thought her neighbor was a **bore**. She loved to invite her over and play with her every chance she got.   Expect   Not Expect

4. Sean bought a painting that he wanted to hang in his room. Sean used a drill to **bore** a hole in the wall.   Expect   Not Expect

5. Karen thinks her older cousin Tommy is a **bore**. She does not like to spend time with him.   Expect   Not Expect

6. The construction worker had to **bore** a hole in the ground. This required him to fill the hole with dirt.   Expect   Not Expect

7. Jessica Sims was a pioneer woman who **bore** one child in the spring. She never gave birth but took one child in to live with her.   Expect   Not Expect

8. Mr. Sims **bore** the weight of the piano on moving day. Mr. Sims pointed out where the piano was to go but did not participate in moving it.   Expect   Not Expect

Create Stories

On a sheet of paper, write a short story or scenario for each of the four meanings of **bore**.

| # Charm

Pre-Lesson Activity—Meanings of Related Words

1   One meaning of **charm** includes the following related words.

   a.   **Grace** can mean the <u>quality of behaving in an attractive and pleasant way</u>. For example, "Even though Celeste did not win the spelling bee, she accepted the second-place ribbon with **grace** and style."
   Write a sentence using **grace**.

   _____

   _____

   b.   **Charisma** can mean the <u>quality of behaving in an attractive and enthusiastic way</u>. For example, "Her **charisma** made her a popular guest at most parties."
   Write a sentence using **charisma**.

   _____

   _____

   c.   To **allure** means to <u>attract</u> something. For example, "Sahara had to **allure** her guests by being friendly and gracious."
   Write a sentence using **allure**.

   _____

   _____

2   A second meaning of **charm** includes the following related words.

   a.   An **ornament** can be a <u>small piece of jewelry</u> such as that worn on a bracelet. For example, "My sister gave her a beautiful silver necklace with a lovely gem **ornament** attached to it."
   Write a sentence using **ornament**.

   _____

   _____

   b.   A **trinket** can mean a <u>small piece of jewelry</u>. For example, "My grandfather bought me a lovely **trinket** on his trip to Australia."
   Write a sentence using **trinket**.

   _____

   _____

c. A **keepsake** can mean a <u>small piece of jewelry</u> given to remember someone by. For example, "Jesse gave his grandmother a **keepsake** that she pinned to her sweater." Write a sentence using **keepsake**.

_____

_____

3 A third meaning of **charm** includes the following related words.

a. A **rabbit's foot** is a <u>lucky object</u> thought to cause good things to happen to people. For example, "My brother carried a **rabbit's foot** on his keychain to bring him good luck." Write a sentence using **rabbit's foot**.

_____

_____

b. A **good-luck piece** is a <u>lucky object</u> thought to have magical powers. For example, "Brendan carried a **good-luck piece** in his pocket during baseball games because he said it made him hit the ball better." Write a sentence using **good-luck piece**.

_____

_____

c. A **talisman** is a <u>lucky object</u> thought to bring success to the person who owns it. For example, "The elderly man carried a **talisman** with him to keep him safe and to bring him good luck on his journeys." Write a sentence using **talisman**.

_____

_____

4 A fourth meaning of **charm** includes the following related words.

a. An **incantation** is a <u>spell</u> that is spoken or sung. For example, "The evil witch said an **incantation** that turned the king into a mouse." Write a sentence using **incantation**.

_____

_____

b. **Sorcery** means <u>casting spells</u> that have supposed magical powers. For example, "The **sorcery** done by the wicked witch caused problems in the magical kingdom." Write a sentence using **sorcery**.

_____

_____

c. **Conjure** can mean to <u>cast a spell</u> on someone. For example, "The boy went to wizardry school and learned how to **conjure** evil spirits." Write a sentence using **conjure**.

_____

_____

Word Meaning in Context

Charm began in the Old French language as a word meaning "song."
Later, in the English language, this meaning expanded to include four
current meanings:

- ❑ **quality of behaving in an attractive way or to attract**
- ❑ **small piece of jewelry**
- ❑ **lucky object**
- ❑ **spell or to cast a spell**

1. The fairy godmother's magic **charm** turned the prince's pot of beans into a pot of gold. The
fairy tried to **charm** the pumpkin into a fancy coach for the princess.

Which of the meanings of **charm** are these? _____

_____

2. Deb is a young woman of great **charm** and beauty. Delia had to **charm** the judges during the
talent competition.

Which of the meanings of **charm** are these? _____

_____

3. Pat wore a **charm** around her neck that was given to her by her mother.

Which of the meanings of **charm** is this?_____

_____

4. Kiera described her four-leaf clover as a "lucky **charm**."

Which of the meanings of **charm** is this?_____

_____

Word Meaning Map   The teacher will give you the **Charm** worksheet.

Complete Each Definition

1. A **charm** can mean the quality of behaving in an _____
way or to attract.

2. A **charm** can also mean a small piece of _____.

3. A **charm** can also mean a _____ object such as
a four-leaf clover.

4. A **charm** can also mean a _____ or to cast a
spell like a fairy godmother does.

Understanding Check

Circle whether **charm** is used as you would expect.

1. Darion thought the new baseball cap he was wearing was a good-luck **charm** after he fell and broke his arm in his backyard.　　Expect　　Not Expect

2. Vickie admired her grandmother who lived in another state. Vickie's grandmother gave her a special **charm** bracelet to keep.　　Expect　　Not Expect

3. Harley always seemed to find things on the ground. Harley thought the new penny he found would make a perfect good-luck **charm**.　　Expect　　Not Expect

4. The talent contest was held in June every year. The judges at the talent contest mentioned how much they liked Amanda's **charm**.　　Expect　　Not Expect

5. The witch had to **charm** the prince. This meant that she had to give him what he wished for in return for him being nice to her.　　Expect　　Not Expect

6. The **charm** on Sela's backpack was broken. Sela asked her mother to fix the zipper because hers had fallen apart.　　Expect　　Not Expect

7. The wicked witch placed a **charm** on the poor prince and turned him into a toad.　　Expect　　Not Expect

8. The young man had to **charm** the parents of his new girlfriend. He told them stories of how many fights he had gotten into and how bad his grades were.　　Expect　　Not Expect

Create Stories

On a sheet of paper, write a short story or scenario for each of the four meanings of **charm**.

Pre-Lesson Activity—Meanings of Related Words

1 One meaning of **dawn** includes the following related words.

a. **Daybreak** is the period in <u>early morning</u> when light from the sun begins to appear in the sky. For example, "Jordan woke at **daybreak** because she was so excited about the first day of school."

Write a sentence using **daybreak**.

_____

_____

b. **Sunrise** is the first appearance of light in the <u>early morning</u>. For example, "Tony liked to get an early start on jogging, so he woke up at **sunrise**."

Write a sentence using **sunrise**.

_____

_____

c. **Sunup** is the period in the <u>early morning</u> when the sun begins to rise in the sky. For example, "The rooster on my grandfather's farm began to crow at **sunup**."

Write a sentence using **sunup**.

_____

_____

2 A second meaning of **dawn** includes the following related words.

a. **Commencement** can mean the <u>beginning</u> of something. For example, "We arrived at the awards dinner before the **commencement** of the ceremonies."

Write a sentence using **commencement**.

_____

_____

b. **Birth** can mean the <u>beginning</u> of something. For example, "The **birth** of the computer age has changed how we do many of the things in our lives."

Write a sentence using **birth**.

_____

_____

c. **Advent** can mean the <u>beginning</u> of something. For example, "The **advent** of cell phones has occurred because people like the convenience of talking to others whenever they wish."

Write a sentence using **advent**.

_____

_____

3 A third meaning of **dawn** includes the following related words.

a. **Occur to** can mean to <u>realize</u> something. For example, "It began to **occur to** her that school would be much tougher than she thought."

Write a sentence using **occur to**.

_____

_____

b. **Strike** can mean to <u>realize</u> something. For example, "Lydia said it began to **strike** her that getting up earlier to go to school would be better than always being late."

Write a sentence using **strike**.

_____

_____

c. **Appear** can mean to <u>realize</u> something. For example, "Cassidy told her friend that the right thing to do would **appear** to her before the day was through."

Write a sentence using **appear**.

_____

_____

Word Meaning in Context

Dawn began in the Old English language as a word meaning "the emergence of day from night." Later, this meaning expanded to include three current meanings:

- ❑ **early morning**
- ❑ **beginning**
- ❑ **realize**

1. It began to **dawn** on Addison that if he wanted to play with his friends he had to get his chores done first.

Which of the meanings of **dawn** is this?_____

_____

2. We woke at **dawn** on our campout so we would have the entire day to hike.

Which of the meanings of **dawn** is this?_____

_____

3. The **dawn** of the Roman Empire will be studied during history class.

Which of the meanings of **dawn** is this?_____

_____

Word Meaning Map   The teacher will give you the **Dawn** worksheet.

Complete Each Definition

1. **Dawn** can mean what happens in early _____ when light from the sun starts to appear in the sky.

2. **Dawn** can also mean the _____ or start of something.

3. **Dawn** can also mean you become aware or _____ something.

Understanding Check

Circle whether **dawn** is used as you would expect.

1. Melissa and Andrea were excited about the **dawn** of another season of basketball. There were no other games to be played until next year.   Expect   Not Expect

2. It did not **dawn** on her that her jacket was unzipped. She stood there and shivered while she waited for the bus.   Expect   Not Expect

3. When Chris and his father go fishing, they get up before **dawn**. They have to drive for two hours to reach their favorite lake before 7 o'clock in the morning.   Expect   Not Expect

4. The streetlights were not on during the day because there was bright sunshine. It was before **dawn**.   Expect   Not Expect

5. Rae provided the correct answer to the teacher's question. The correct answer did not **dawn** on her.   Expect   Not Expect

6. Lee and the other players had to get a physical exam before they played football. It was the **dawn** of the football season.   Expect   Not Expect

Create Stories

On a sheet of paper, write a short story or scenario for each of the three meanings of **dawn**.

Deposit

Pre-Lesson Activity—Meanings of Related Words

1 One meaning of **deposit** includes the following related words.

a. To **set something down** means to <u>put or place</u> it in a certain position or location. For example, "Please **set** the watch **down** on the counter where it belongs."

Write a sentence using **set down**.

_____

_____

b. To **leave** something is to <u>put or place</u> it somewhere and not take it with you when you go. For example, "Marvin was told to **leave** his small pocketknife at home when he went to the airport because of the increased security."

Write a sentence using **leave**.

_____

_____

c. To **drop** something can mean to <u>put or place</u> it somewhere. For example, "Melissa's mother asked her to **drop** the letter in the mailbox on her way to school."

Write a sentence using **drop**.

_____

_____

2 A second meaning of **deposit** includes the following related words.

a. **Installment** can mean <u>sums of money</u> that are paid at certain points in time. For example, "Wilson made the first **installment** payment on his new car."

Write a sentence using **installment**.

_____

_____

b. A **down payment** is a <u>sum of money</u> that is a partial payment for something. For example, "Jo provided a **down payment** on the in-ground swimming pool she was having installed in her backyard."

Write a sentence using **down payment**.

_____

_____

c. A **payment** is a <u>sum of money</u> given to buy something. For example, "Josh saved enough money to make a **payment** on the mountain bike he wanted at the bike shop."

Write a sentence using **payment**.

_____

_____

3   A third meaning of **deposit** includes the following related words.

a. **Residue** is an <u>accumulation or vein of material</u> that remains after the main part of something has gone or has been taken away. For example, "The soap **residue** left on my car after I washed it made it look cloudy and dirty."

Write a sentence using **residue**.

_____

_____

b. **Sediment** is an <u>accumulation or vein of material</u> that settles on the bottom of a liquid. For example, "Mabel filled the jar with water from the creek and noticed the **sediment** that lined the bottom of the jar when she was through.

Write a sentence using **sediment**.

_____

_____

c. **Dregs** can mean an <u>accumulation or vein of material</u> that is left after something is gone. For example, "Sherri was all out of lemonade. Only the **dregs** were left at the bottom of the pitcher."

Write a sentence using **dregs**.

_____

_____

Word Meaning in Context

Deposit began in the Latin language as a word meaning "lay aside or put down." Later, in the English language, this meaning expanded to include three current meanings:

- ❏ **put or place**
- ❏ **sum of money**
- ❏ **accumulation or vein of material**

1. There is a rich **deposit** of iron ore near the city where Kayla and her family live.

Which of the meanings of **deposit** is this?_____

_____

2. Tyler's mother wanted him to **deposit** his backpack on the counter when he came home from school.

Which of the meanings of **deposit** is this?_____

_____

3. To open a savings account at the bank, Elizabeth learned that she needed to make a minimum **deposit** of $100.

Which of the meanings of **deposit** is this?_____

_____

Word Meaning Map   The teacher will give you the **Deposit** worksheet.

Complete Each Definition

1. **Deposit** can mean to _____
or place something somewhere.

2. **Deposit** can also mean a sum of _____
that you put in the bank for safe keeping.

3. **Deposit** can also mean a substance or _____
that you find in or on the ground or some other location.

 **Understanding Check**

Circle whether **deposit** is used as you would expect.

1. Daniel made a **deposit** with the money that he earned from mowing lawns. His bank account had forty dollars less in it after the deposit.

   Expect   Not Expect

2. Alexis made a weekly **deposit** at the bank with the money she received from her baby-sitting jobs. She now had enough money in the bank to buy the bicycle that she wanted.

   Expect   Not Expect

3. During their geology unit, Nicholas and his class took an exciting field trip to see a rich **deposit** of oil shale or rock.

   Expect   Not Expect

4. Abigail and her friends would always **deposit** their coats on the hooks in the hallway before coming into the classroom.

   Expect   Not Expect

5. The flood left the streets clean and clear. It left a **deposit** of mud in the street.

   Expect   Not Expect

6. Kelly's teacher said to **deposit** the book in the drop box at the library. Kelly did as she was told and set it on the ground near the drop box.

   Expect   Not Expect

Create Stories

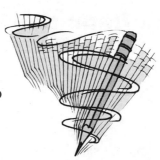

On a sheet of paper, write a short story or scenario for each of the three meanings of **deposit**.

Diamond

Pre-Lesson Activity—Meanings of Related Words

1 One meaning of **diamond** includes the following related words.

a. An **infield** is the part of the <u>baseball field</u> that is marked off by three bases and home plate. For example, "The baseball players ran out of the dugout and lined up on the **infield**."

Write a sentence using **infield**.

_____

_____

b. A **ballpark** is a place that has a <u>baseball field</u>. For example, "We love going to the **ballpark** to watch the Spokane Indians play baseball on a Friday night."

Write a sentence using **ballpark**.

_____

_____

c. A **playing field** is a dirt or grass area that can be used as a <u>baseball field</u>. For example, "Jess went to the **playing field** with his bat, ball, and glove hoping to see his friends there so he could play baseball."

Write a sentence using **playing field**.

_____

_____

2 A second meaning of **diamond** includes the following related words.

a. A **gem** can be a <u>precious, hard stone</u> that is often worn as jewelry. For example, "Helene's boyfriend bought her a **gem** after they had been dating for two years."

Write a sentence using **gem**.

_____

_____

b. A **jewel** can be a <u>precious, hard stone</u> that is often worn as jewelry. For example, "Hannah's mother had an antique pin that had a lovely **jewel** in it."

Write a sentence using **jewel**.

_____

_____

c. A **rock** can be a <u>precious, hard stone</u> that is often worn as jewelry. For example, "When Cleo's friends saw the ring Bryan had given her, they said, 'What a **rock**' to describe the large stone in it."

Write a sentence using **rock**.

_____

_____

3 A third meaning of **diamond** has no related words.

a. When **diamond** is used in this way, it means a <u>figure with four equal sides shaped like a kite</u>. For example, "Mr. Parks asked the class to color the diamond shape blue."

Write a sentence using **diamond**.

_____

_____

Word Meaning in Context

Diamond began in the Latin and Greek languages as a word meaning "hardest imaginable substance." Later, in the English language, this meaning expanded to include three current meanings:

- ❏ **baseball field**
- ❏ **precious, hard stone**
- ❏ **figure with four equal sides shaped like a kite**

1. *Black Beauty*, a famous horse story written by Anna Sewell, features a black horse with a white **diamond** on his forehead.

Which of the meanings of **diamond** is this? _____

_____

2. Alexander loved to go to the **diamond** for batting practice.

Which of the meanings of **diamond** is this? _____

_____

3. Lauren received a **diamond** necklace from her grandmother on her birthday.

Which of the meanings of **diamond** is this? _____

_____

Word Meaning Map   The teacher will give you the **Diamond** worksheet.

Complete Each Definition

1. A **diamond** can mean a _____
field where baseball is played.

2. A **diamond** can also mean an extremely hard and precious _____
that is used in jewelry.

3. A **diamond** can also mean a _____
with four equal sides shaped like a kite.

✔ Understanding Check

Circle whether **diamond** is used as you would expect.

1. Daniel enjoyed meeting his friends at the **diamond** after school. Daniel liked playing shortstop.

Expect   Not Expect

2. Jessica thought her mother's **diamond** ring was beautiful. Jessica wanted a ring just like it when she grew up.

Expect   Not Expect

3. Taylor and his friends had tickets for the ice hockey game. They were really looking forward to going to the **diamond**.

Expect   Not Expect

4. The art teacher instructed Christopher to cut his construction paper into a **diamond** shape. The shape Christopher cut looked like a kite.

Expect   Not Expect

5. Marissa bought a necklace with a stone in it at the local mall for her friend's birthday. The necklace was expensive since it had a real **diamond**.

Expect   Not Expect

6. Monique drew a round shape on her paper. Everyone said it was a **diamond**.

Expect   Not Expect

Create Stories

On a sheet of paper, write a short story or scenario for each of the three meanings of **diamond**.

TARGET WORD |

Pre-Lesson Activity—Meanings of Related Words

1 One meaning of **dip** includes the following related words.

   a. **Immerse** can mean to <u>plunge or drop</u> or put something completely under the surface of something else. For example, "Bonnie had to **immerse** her head under running water to wash the shampoo out of it."

     Write a sentence using **immerse**.

     _____

     _____

   b. **Descend** can mean to <u>plunge or drop</u> or lower something. For example, "Anna watched the moon **descend** behind the trees as she sat on her back porch."

     Write a sentence using **descend**.

     _____

     _____

   c. **Depression** can mean a <u>plunge or drop</u> in something. For example, "There was a **depression** in the road that we avoided because we did not want to crash our bikes."

     Write a sentence using **depression**.

     _____

     _____

2 A second meaning of **dip** includes the following related words.

   a. **Dish out** can mean to <u>scoop</u> something such as soup or ice cream. For example, "Timon asked the waiter to **dish out** two scoops of fudge marble ice cream."

     Write a sentence using **dish out**.

     _____

     _____

b. **Ladle** can mean to <u>scoop</u> something, such as soup, into a bowl. For example, "Jamal asked his grandmother for another **ladle** of soup because he was so hungry."

Write a sentence using **ladle**.

_____

_____

c. **Bail** can mean to <u>scoop</u> something out of something else. For example, "Jackson had to **bail** water out of his boat with a bucket because it was starting to sink."

Write a sentence using **bail**.

_____

_____

3 A third meaning of **dip** has no related words.

a. When **dip** is used in this way, it means <u>sauce or soft mixture used to dunk other foods in</u> often served at parties. For example, "At the house-warming party, Mr. and Mrs. Stockman served crackers and **dip** along with fresh fruit and vegetables."

Write a sentence using **dip**.

_____

_____

Word Meaning in Context

Dip began in the Old German language as a word meaning "deep or hollow." Later, in the English language, this meaning expanded to include three current meanings:

- ❏ **plunge or drop**
- ❏ **scoop**
- ❏ **sauce or soft mixture used to dunk other foods in**

1. Will served guacamole **dip** and chips during the party.

   Which of the meanings of **dip** is this? _____

   _____

2. Sarah had to **dip** her finger in cold water after she burned it to reduce the pain she felt. Sela took a **dip** in the lake before going to school. Joe saw a **dip** in the road head of him.

   Which of the meanings of **dip** are these? _____

   _____

3. Megan had to **dip** the clam chowder into individual serving bowls for her guests.

   Which of the meanings of **dip** is this? _____

   _____

Word Meaning Map   The teacher will give you the **Dip** worksheet.

Complete Each Definition

1. **Dip** can mean to plunge or _____
   into something, such as water, or a drop or a plunge in the surface of something.

2. **Dip** can also mean to _____
   something such as soup.

3. **Dip** can also mean a _____ or soft mixture
   used to dunk other foods in.

Understanding Check

Circle whether **dip** is used as you would expect.

1. While riding the school bus, both Brianna and William noticed that there was a **dip** in the road ahead. Their stomachs always bounced when the bus went over this part of the road.   Expect   Not Expect

2. Jessica said she wanted to take a **dip** in the ocean. This involved standing on shore and feeling the mist from the waves hit her face.   Expect   Not Expect

3. Jim ordered **dip** with his chips. He wanted chips and a pickle.   Expect   Not Expect

4. Marge was preparing for her guests. She set out carrots and celery as well as a creamy **dip** made with sour cream and spices.   Expect   Not Expect

5. Yolanda's father asked for more soup at the restaurant. The waitress said she would **dip** some more soup in his bowl.   Expect   Not Expect

6. The soup was not eaten by anyone. Wendy said she took a **dip** of it and ate it from a soup bowl.   Expect   Not Expect

Create Stories

On a sheet of paper, write a short story or scenario for each of the three meanings of **dip**.

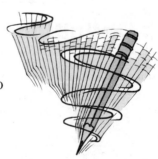

Dressing

Pre-Lesson Activity—Meanings of Related Words

1 One meaning of **dressing** includes the following related words.

a. **Trimming** can mean <u>something put on</u> something else. For example, "Frank liked the **trimming** on the windows of the market down the street." Write a sentence using **trimming**.

_____

_____

b. **Clothing** can mean <u>to put on something</u>. For example, "When asked what she was doing in her room, Becca replied, 'I am **clothing** myself.'" Write a sentence using **clothing**.

_____

_____

c. **Display** can mean <u>something put on</u>. For example, "Wendell liked the window **display** in the Christmas store at the mall." Write a sentence using **display**.

_____

_____

2 A second meaning of **dressing** includes the following related words.

a. **Vinaigrette** is a <u>seasoned mixture</u> of oil and vinegar that is put on salads. For example, "Andy ordered **vinaigrette** for his salad at the restaurant." Write a sentence using **vinaigrette**.

_____

_____

b. **Stuffing** can mean a <u>seasoned mixture</u> used to stuff meats such as turkey or vegetables. For example, "My mother makes the best cornbread **stuffing** in the world at Thanksgiving." Write a sentence using **stuffing**.

_____

_____

c. **Salad topping** is a <u>seasoned mixture</u> of oils and other things that is put on food such as salads and sandwiches. For example, "Zoe loved **salad topping** so much that she dipped her french fries in it." Write a sentence using **salad topping**.

_____

_____

3 A third meaning of **dressing** includes the following related words.

a. A **compress** can mean a protective <u>covering for a wound</u>. For example, "Ruth put a cold **compress** on her daughter's arm to stop the swelling."
Write a sentence using **compress**.

_____

_____

b. A **bandage** is a protective <u>covering for a wound</u>. For example, "Vivian had to wear a **bandage** on her injured arm after she fell from her bike."
Write a sentence using **bandage**.

_____

_____

c. **Band-Aid**© is a protective <u>covering for a wound</u>. For example, "The nurse put a **Band-Aid** on her finger after she accidently cut it with a knife."
Write a sentence using **Band-Aid**.

_____

_____

4 A fourth meaning of **dressing** includes the following related words.

a. **Curling** can mean <u>fixing</u> your hair in a particular way. For example, "My hairstylist loved **curling** my sister's hair because it was so easy to do and looked so pretty."
Write a sentence using **curling**.

_____

_____

b. **Grooming** can mean <u>fixing</u> your hair in a particular way. For example, "Her brother spent a great deal of time **grooming** his hair for the big dance that evening."
Write a sentence using **grooming**.

_____

_____

c. **Doing up** can mean <u>fixing</u> your hair in a particular way. For example, "All the cheerleaders came over to my house. We spent time **doing up** each other's hair."
Write a sentence using **doing up**.

_____

_____

Word Meaning in Context

Dressing began in the Old French language as a word meaning "put right or put straight." Later, in the English language, this meaning changed to include four current meanings:

- ❑ **something put on or to put on something**
- ❑ **seasoned mixture**
- ❑ **covering for a wound**
- ❑ **fixing**

1. Sally spent a great deal of time **dressing** her hair.

Which of the meanings of **dressing** is this? _____

_____

2. The window **dressing** was tastefully done for the holidays and included two reindeer and Santa Claus in his sled. Nicole didn't spend much time **dressing** for school because she got up late.

Which of the meanings of **dressing** are these? _____

_____

3. David loved blue cheese **dressing** on his salad.

Which of the meanings of **dressing** is this? _____

_____

4. Benjamin needed a **dressing** for the cut on his knee.

Which of the meanings of **dressing** is this? _____

_____

Word Meaning Map   The teacher will give you the **Dressing** worksheet.

Complete Each Definition

1. Dressing can mean a seasoned _____
of oils and other things used for salads or as a stuffing.

2. Dressing can also mean a protective _____
or bandage for a wound.

3. Dressing can also mean _____
something such as your hair.

4. Dressing can also mean something put on or to put on _____
such as clothes.

Understanding Check

Circle whether **dressing** is used as you would expect.

1. Justin liked the **dressing** his mother served on Thanksgiving. She usually put it inside the turkey to add to its flavoring.

   Expect   Not Expect

2. Grace was still **dressing** when her friend Rachel arrived to walk with her to school. It always took her a long time to put on her clothes.

   Expect   Not Expect

3. Ryan took riding lessons once a month. Ryan fell off his horse and needed a **dressing** for the cut on his arm. This would help it to heal faster.

   Expect   Not Expect

4. Jasmine's favorite part of supper was salad. Jasmine liked **dressing** on her salad. She always ate her salad plain, with just lettuce, tomatoes, and croutons.

   Expect   Not Expect

5. The window **dressing** was completed by Martin's father. He carefully washed the window and did not put any displays or pictures on it.

   Expect   Not Expect

6. Bonita played with her cousins all day without getting hurt. She needed a **dressing** on her knee to keep it protected from dirt.

   Expect   Not Expect

7. Harold always went to school with his hair messed up and his clothes looking wrinkled. He spent time **dressing** his hair each morning.

   Expect   Not Expect

8. Kent wanted to become a hair stylist. He loved **dressing** his friends' hair and they always loved what they looked like when he was finished.

   Expect   Not Expect

Create Stories

On a sheet of paper, write a short story or scenario for each of the four meanings of **dressing**.

 **Ease**

 ## Pre-Lesson Activity—Meanings of Related Words

1 One meaning of **ease** includes the following related words.

a. **Effortlessness** means to <u>do something without difficulty</u> or with little or no effort. For example, "When Seth played basketball, he exuded a natural **effortlessness**." Write a sentence using **effortlessness**.

_____

_____

b. **Facility** can mean that you can <u>do something without difficulty</u>. For example, "Having been raised in Europe, Caroline spoke German and French with **facility**." Write a sentence using **facility**.

_____

_____

c. **Fluency** means one can <u>do something without difficulty</u>. For example, "The **fluency** of his guitar playing surprised Spencer." Write a sentence using **fluency**.

_____

_____

2 A second meaning of **ease** includes the following related words.

a. **Relieve** can mean to <u>reduce a problem</u>. For example, "The government sent emergency food aid to help **relieve** the famine in Africa." Write a sentence using **relieve**.

_____

_____

b. **Alleviate** means to <u>reduce a problem</u> and make it less intense or severe. For example, "The medicine that Taylor took helped **alleviate** her headache." Write a sentence using **alleviate**.

_____

_____

c. **Lessen** can mean to <u>reduce a problem</u> or lower something. For example, "A healthy diet and plenty of exercise can **lessen** the risk of getting sick." Write a sentence using **lessen**.

_____

_____

3 A third meaning of **ease** includes the following related words.

a. **Edge** can mean to <u>move carefully</u> and slowly. For example, "Molly tried to **edge** closer to the front of the line so she could stand next to her friends."

Write a sentence using **edge**.

_____

_____

b. **Slide** can mean to <u>move carefully</u> and smoothly. For example, "Martin tried to **slide** the refrigerator back against the wall after cleaning behind it."

Write a sentence using **slide**.

_____

_____

c. **Slip** can mean to <u>move carefully</u> and gently. For example, "Joe tried to **slip** the halter on the frightened horse's head so he could put him back in the corral."

Write a sentence using **slip**.

_____

_____

4 A fourth meaning of **ease** includes the following related words.

a. **Leisure** can mean a time when you have no work to do and can enjoy <u>comfort and security</u>. For example, "Vincent dreamed of the day he would be rich so he could live a life of **leisure**."

Write a sentence using **leisure**.

_____

_____

b. **Relaxation** means that one is experiencing <u>comfort and security</u> with little stress. For example, "**Relaxation** and little worry in our lives is a goal we all hope to achieve."

Write a sentence using **relaxation**.

_____

_____

c. **Luxury** can mean living in great <u>comfort and security</u>, among nice surroundings. For example, "Lucas thought the new family in the neighborhood lived a life of **luxury** because they had such a nice house."

Write a sentence using **luxury**.

_____

_____

Word Meaning in Context

Ease began in the Old French language as a word meaning "comfort or pleasure." Later, in the English language, this meaning expanded to include four current meanings:

- ❏ **do something without difficulty**
- ❏ **reduce a problem**
- ❏ **move carefully**
- ❏ **comfort and security**

1. Samuel's uncle felt more at **ease** when he quit his job and became a gardener.

Which of the meanings of **ease** is this? _____

_____

2. They put the dinosaur bones into special containers for **ease** of transportation.

Which of the meanings of **ease** is this? _____

_____

3. To **ease** the problem of children bullying others on the playground, more teacher supervision is needed.

Which of the meanings of **ease** is this? _____

_____

4. Please **ease** your way down the bridge so you don't fall into the river.

Which of the meanings of **ease** is this? _____

_____

Word Meaning Map   The teacher will give you the **Ease** worksheet.

Complete Each Definition

1. **Ease** can mean to _____ a problem and make it less severe or intense.

2. **Ease** can also mean to move something slowly and _____.

3. **Ease** can also mean that things are going well for you and that you feel _____ and security.

4. **Ease** can also mean to do something without _____.

✔ Understanding Check

Circle whether **ease** is used as you would expect.

1. Every summer Samuel and his family went on a vacation to the mountains. Samuel felt at **ease** while he was on vacation. Expect   Not Expect

2. The playground was littered with garbage one morning. Isabella suggested one way to **ease** the problem of littering was to place more trash cans in the area. Expect   Not Expect

3. Hunter and his brother had to **ease** the new TV set through the front door. They wanted to make sure that they did not break it. Expect   Not Expect

4. Robert said he did not feel at **ease** in large groups of people. He loved to attend big community gatherings where he did not know anyone. Expect   Not Expect

5. Stephanie ran the one-mile race with **ease** compared to the other runners. She found it hard and difficult to complete in the time allotted. Expect   Not Expect

6. To get his bike to fit into the garage Brandon had to **ease** it into a narrow space. He opened the door and shoved it in quickly. Expect   Not Expect

7. Jorge wanted to **ease** the problem of noise pollution in his community. He decided to bring his boom box outside so he could listen to loud music. Expect   Not Expect

8. Erika was excellent at playing the piano. She played it with **ease**. Expect   Not Expect

Create Stories

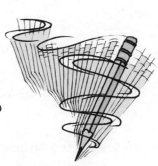

On a sheet of paper, write a short story or scenario for each of the four meanings of **ease**.

Entrance

Pre-Lesson Activity—Meanings of Related Words

1 One meaning of **entrance** includes the following related words.

    a. **Portal** can mean the <u>place of entry</u> into somewhere. For example, "The castle had only one **portal**."

       Write a sentence using **portal**.

       _____

       _____

    b. **Door** can mean the <u>place of entry</u> into a building, room, or location. For example, "It was quicker for Leah to use the side **door** to get to her first class of the day."

       Write a sentence using **door**.

       _____

       _____

    c. **Gate** can mean a structure like a door that swings to open and close and is the <u>place of entry</u> to somewhere. For example, "Jonathan left the zoo through the main **gate**."

       Write a sentence using **gate**.

       _____

       _____

2 A second meaning of **entrance** includes the following related words.

    a. **Arrival** can mean the act of <u>making an appearance</u>. For example, "Everyone welcomed the soldier's **arrival** after he had been away to war."

       Write a sentence using **arrival**.

       _____

       _____

b. **Entry** can mean the act of entering a room or <u>making an appearance</u>. For example, "Robert's **entry** drew a lot of attention at the birthday party because he was wearing a funny hat."

Write a sentence using **entry**.

_____

_____

c. **Emergence** can mean the act of entering a location or <u>making an appearance</u>. For example, "Her fans cheered Courtney's **emergence** at the rock concert on Friday night."

Write a sentence using **emergence**.

_____

_____

3 A third meaning of **entrance** includes the following related words.

a. **Access** can mean that you have <u>permission to join</u> a group or activity. For example, "William wanted to gain **access** to the swimming pool and health club because his friends spent a lot of time there."

Write a sentence using **access**.

_____

_____

b. **Admission** can mean that someone is given <u>permission to join</u> a group or activity. For example, "**Admission** to the chess tournament will be by invitation only."

Write a sentence using **admission**.

_____

_____

c. **Acceptance** can mean that you have <u>permission to join</u> a group or activity. For example, "Becky's **acceptance** into the honor roll club made her very happy because she had studied hard during the first semester."

Write a sentence using **acceptance**.

_____

_____

Word Meaning in Context

Entrance began in the Old French language as a word meaning "within." Later, in the English language, this meaning expanded to include three current meanings:

- ❏ **place of entry**
- ❏ **making an appearance**
- ❏ **permission to join**

1. Nathaniel's older brother gained **entrance** to medical school.

Which of the meanings of **entrance** is this? _____

_____

2. Connor and Luke waited at the **entrance** of the stadium for their friends.

Which of the meanings of **entrance** is this? _____

_____

3. Sophia made a grand **entrance** onto the stage during the school play.

Which of the meanings of **entrance** is this? _____

_____

Word Meaning Map   The teacher will give you the **Entrance** worksheet.

Complete Each Definition

1. **Entrance** can mean the place of _____
into a room or location.

2. **Entrance** can also mean the act of making an _____
into a building or place.

3. **Entrance** can also mean _____ to join a group
or activity.

✔ Understanding Check

Circle whether **entrance** is used as you would expect.

1. Amber stood at the **entrance** of the library to wait for her friends. They were going to study together.　　Expect　　Not Expect

2. When the governor came to visit our school, he made a grand **entrance** into the auditorium. No one noticed that the governor had been at the school.　　Expect　　Not Expect

3. Wendy was late to school one day. She wanted to make a quiet **entrance** into her classroom.　　Expect　　Not Expect

4. Jordan was allowed **entrance** into a special math program because his grades were very good in math. Naturally, math was his favorite subject.　　Expect　　Not Expect

5. The main **entrance** to the front of the school building faces the street. Kyle had to go around to the back of the building to get in each morning.　　Expect　　Not Expect

6. Les joined the Boy's Club to play basketball with his friends. He was not allowed **entrance** to the club.　　Expect　　Not Expect

Create Stories

On a sheet of paper, write a short story or scenario for each of the three meanings of **entrance**.

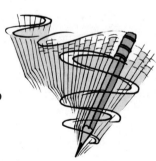

 Pre-Lesson Activity—Meanings of Related Words

1 One meaning of **figure** includes the following related words.

a. **Form** can mean the <u>shape</u> or appearance of someone. For example, "Regular exercise, a healthy diet, and plenty of sleep were the reasons Shara had a slender **form**." Write a sentence using **form**.

_____

_____

b. **Silhouette** can mean a dark <u>shape</u> seen against a light background. For example, "In art class, Tiffany painted the **silhouette** of the city skyline at sunset." Write a sentence using **silhouette**.

_____

_____

c. **Outline** can mean the main <u>shape</u> or edge of something without any details. For example, "Christian was instructed to draw a simple **outline** of his house." Write a sentence using **outline**.

_____

_____

2 A second meaning of **figure** includes the following related words.

a. **Numeral** can mean a symbol that represents a <u>number or amount</u>. For example, "The **numeral** '7' stands for seven." Write a sentence using **numeral**.

_____

_____

b. **Sum** can mean the <u>number or amount</u> that is obtained when two or more numbers are added together. For example, "When the salaries of the football and basketball coaches are added together it comes to a very high **sum**." Write a sentence using **sum**.

_____

_____

c. **Digit** can mean a <u>number or amount</u> from 0 to 9. For example, "The number '7' contains one **digit**." Write a sentence using **digit**.

_____

_____

3 A third meaning of **figure** includes the following related words.

a. **Leader** can mean a <u>person</u> who is in charge of something. For example, "The mayor is an important **leader** in the city."

Write a sentence using **leader**.

_____

_____

b. **Celebrity** can mean a <u>person</u> who is famous. For example, "Christina became a notable **celebrity** when she saved a friend from drowning."

Write a sentence using **celebrity**.

_____

_____

c. **Dignitary** can mean a <u>person</u> who has an important position in a society. For example, "A United States senator is considered an influential **dignitary**."

Write a sentence using **dignitary**.

_____

_____

4 A fourth meaning of **figure** includes the following related words.

a. **Think** can mean to <u>decide or estimate</u> about something. For example, "Erik said, 'I **think** it will take ten hours to drive to the mountains .'"

Write a sentence using **think**.

_____

_____

b. **Calculate** can mean to <u>decide or estimate</u> carefully about something. For example, "Heather wanted to **calcuate** a way to sell enough food for the school fundraiser to earn a nice prize."

Write a sentence using **calcuate**.

_____

_____

c. **Imagine** can mean to <u>decide or estimate</u> that something is probably true. For example, "Margaret said, 'I do not **imagine** that my homework will take me very long to complete.'"

Write a sentence using **imagine**.

_____

_____

Word Meaning in Context

Figure began in the Old French language as a word meaning "form and shape." Later, in the English language, this meaning expanded to include four current meanings:

- ❑ **shape**
- ❑ **number or amount**
- ❑ **person**
- ❑ **decide or estimate**

1. Rico had to **figure** out how much paint he would need to cover his room.

Which of the meanings of **figure** is this? _____

_____

2. Richard drew a **figure** with five sides in art class.

Which of the meanings of **figure** is this? _____

_____

3. Jared could not tell whether the **figure** was a three or an eight.

Which of the meanings of **figure** is this? _____

_____

4. Kimberly saw a **figure** standing at the back of the building.

Which of the meanings of **figure** is this? _____

_____

Word Meaning Map   The teacher will give you the **Figure** worksheet.

Complete Each Definition

1. **Figure** can mean the _____ of something.

2. **Figure** can also mean the symbol for a _____ or amount.

3. **Figure** can also mean an important _____ who is famous.

4. **Figure** can also mean to decide or _____ that something will happen.

Understanding Check

Circle whether **figure** is used as you would expect.

1. Steven's father had a job as an armored car driver. The amount of money the armored car carried was a very large **figure**.

   Expect   Not Expect

2. Raymond wanted to **figure** how many lawns he would have to mow to earn enough money to buy a new video game.

   Expect   Not Expect

3. Jade and Trinity were surprised to see a rock star at the grocery store. They were thrilled to see such a famous **figure** in person.

   Expect   Not Expect

4. Veronica wanted to **figure** out a way to help the homeless family on her street. She did not want to do anything to assist them.

   Expect   Not Expect

5. Erin always looked forward to art class. One day she drew a picture with a **figure** of a triangle in the middle of it.

   Expect   Not Expect

6. Samuel liked everything but the shape of his clay art project. He thought its **figure** was perfect.

   Expect   Not Expect

7. Sean lived in a small town and had a school assignment to do a report on an important **figure**. He decided to do a report on his favorite historical place to visit—the White House.

   Expect   Not Expect

8. A sack of fresh apples cost Garret a large **figure**. The store manager gave the apples to him for free.

   Expect   Not Expect

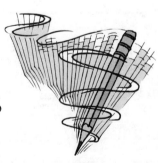

Create Stories

On a sheet of paper, write a short story or scenario for each of the four meanings of **figure**.

Goal

Pre-Lesson Activity—Meanings of Related Words

1 One meaning of **goal** includes the following related words.

    a. **Objective** can mean an <u>aim or purpose</u> that you plan to do or achieve. For example, "Ana's main **objective** is simply to make the basketball team."

    Write a sentence using **objective**.

    _____

    _____

    b. **Target** can mean an <u>aim or purpose</u> that you are trying to achieve. For example, "The school had a **target** for each student to sell ten items during the annual fall fundraiser."

    Write a sentence using **target**.

    _____

    _____

    c. **Intention** can mean an <u>aim or purpose</u> for what you want and plan to do. For example, "Jeremiah's **intention** was to finish his homework by 7:00 p.m. so he could watch his favorite TV show."

    Write a sentence using **intention**.

    _____

    _____

2 A second meaning of **goal** includes the following related words.

    a. **Hoop** can mean a piece of <u>game equipment</u> through which players try to throw a basketball. For example, "Joshua's father made a **hoop** for him in the backyard so he could play basketball."

    Write a sentence using **hoop**.

    _____

    _____

b. **End zone** can mean a <u>place</u> at either end of the playing field into which the football must be carried or passed to score a touchdown. For example, "Jacob crossed into the **end zone** in the fourth quarter to score a touchdown for his team."

Write a sentence using **end zone**.

_____

_____

c. **Net** can mean a piece of <u>game equipment</u> or structure into which one must put a ball or puck in order to score points. For example, "The goalie is the player who stands in front of the **net** and attempts to keep the other team from scoring."

Write a sentence using **net**.

_____

_____

3 A third meaning of **goal** includes the following related words.

a. **Mark** can mean that a person has made a <u>successful attempt at scoring</u> in a game. For example, "Jessica was thrilled she was able to make a **mark** for her team in the final minute of the game."

Write a sentence using **mark**.

_____

_____

b. **Score** can mean to make a <u>successful attempt at scoring</u> in an activity or game. For example, "Matthew's coach was pleased to see him make a **score** in the hockey game on Saturday."

Write a sentence using **score**.

_____

_____

c. **Point** can mean to make a <u>successful attempt at scoring</u> in a game or sport. For example, "The way to make a **point** in basketball is to throw or toss the ball into the basket."

Write a sentence using **point**.

_____

_____

Word Meaning in Context

Goal began in the Old English language as a word meaning the "finishing line of a race." Later, this meaning expanded to include three current meanings:

- ❑ **aim or purpose**
- ❑ **game equipment or place to score points**
- ❑ **successful attempt at scoring**

1. Michael made a **goal** for his team to win the championship.

   Which of the meanings of **goal** is this? _____

   _____

2. Christopher's class had a **goal** to increase their spelling test average during the second semester of school.

   Which of the meanings of **goal** is this? _____

   _____

3. Ashley kicked the ball toward the **goal**.

   Which of the meanings of **goal** is this? _____

   _____

Word Meaning Map   The teacher will give you the **Goal** worksheet.

Complete Each Definition

1. **Goal** can mean an _____ or purpose that you plan to do or hope to achieve.

2. **Goal** can also mean the game _____ or place where the players try to get a ball or puck in order to score points.

3. **Goal** can also mean to make a successful attempt at _____ .

Understanding Check

Circle whether **goal** is used as you would expect.

1. Jacob wanted to practice soccer at home without going to the park. He made a **goal** out of a cardboard box.

   Expect   Not Expect

2. Samantha had a **goal** to earn enough money to purchase a new bike. She did a variety of jobs in the community to accomplish this.

   Expect   Not Expect

3. Emily took her basketball to the park. She was glad when she saw a basketball **goal**. She had nowhere to play so she returned home.

   Expect   Not Expect

4. Andrew wanted to score at least one **goal** during his soccer game. He was thrilled when he scored twice during the game.

   Expect   Not Expect

5. Brittany's **goal** was to have a quiet and relaxing evening. She invited some friends over and they had lots of fun dancing to loud music.

   Expect   Not Expect

6. Amanda made at least one **goal** every game for her soccer team. She was a very good defensive player and had not scored a point for her team all season.

   Expect   Not Expect

Create Stories

On a sheet of paper, write a short story or scenario for each of the three meanings of **goal**.

TARGET WORD | Hash

Pre-Lesson Activity—Meanings of Related Words

1 One meaning of **hash** includes the following related words.

   a. **Mess up** can mean <u>do something badly</u>. For example, "Dean was hoping he wouldn't **mess up** during the school play and forget his lines.

      Write a sentence using **mess up**.

      _____

      _____

   b. **Spoil** can mean <u>do something badly</u>. For example, "Mr. Wilson was throwing a back-yard barbecue and told Dennis to stay on his side of the fence so as not to **spoil** it."

      Write a sentence using **spoil**.

      _____

      _____

   c. **Botch** means <u>do something badly</u>. For example, "Betty was stitching a quilt with her grandmother. She tried to do a good job and not **botch** it."

      Write a sentence using **botch**.

      _____

      _____

2 A second meaning of **hash** includes the following related words.

   a. **Discuss** can mean to <u>talk</u> about. For example, "Alan's father met with his teacher to **discuss** Alan's progress in school."

      Write a sentence using **discuss**.

      _____

      _____

   b. **Speak** means to <u>talk</u>. For example, "Kristen was shy and did not like to speak with strangers."

      Write a sentence using **speak**.

      _____

      _____

c. **Chat** means to <u>talk</u> informally. For example, "Beth loved to call her friends and **chat** for hours on the phone."

Write a sentence using **chat**.

_____

_____

3 A third meaning of **hash** has no related words.

a. When **hash** is used in this way, it means <u>chopped meat mixed with potatoes</u>. For example, "Jimmy cooked so much **hash** that the family would probably be eating it for leftovers the rest of the week."

Write a sentence using **hash**.

_____

_____

4 A fourth meaning of **hash** includes the following related words.

a. **Shred** can mean to <u>cut into small pieces</u>. For example, "We **shred** all of our unwanted mail before we put it in the trash."

Write a sentence using **shred**.

_____

_____

b. **Mince** can mean to <u>cut into small pieces</u>. For example, "My mother likes to **mince** the peppers before she puts them in the salad."

Write a sentence using **mince**.

_____

_____

c. **Chop** can mean to <u>cut into small pieces</u>. For example, "We need to **chop** some potatoes for dinner."

Write a sentence using **chop**.

_____

_____

Word Meaning in Context

Hash began in the Old French language as a word meaning "axe." Later, in the English language, this meaning expanded to include four current meanings:

- ❏ **do something badly**
- ❏ **talk**
- ❏ **chopped meat mixed with potatoes**
- ❏ **cut into small pieces**

1. The first meal Tommy learned how to cook was **hash** because it was so simple to make.

Which of the meanings of **hash** is this? _____

_____

2. Wanda did not know how to build the gingerbread house and ended up making a **hash** of it.

Which of the meanings of **hash** is this? _____

_____

3. After a controversial play, the referees would **hash** it out with the coaches by the sideline.

Which of the meanings of **hash** is this? _____

_____

4. Before he made the stew, Alex had to **hash** the cabbage.

Which of the meanings of **hash** is this? _____

_____

Word Meaning Map   The teacher will give you the **Hash** worksheet.

Complete Each Definition

1. **Hash** can mean to do something _____
or poorly.

2. **Hash** can also mean to _____ into small pieces.

3. **Hash** can also mean to _____ or chat with someone.

4. **Hash** can also mean chopped _____ mixed with potatoes.

Understanding Check

Circle whether **hash** is used as you would expect.

1. After the two boys were caught fighting, the principal told them to sit down and **hash** it out in a more mature way. The boys made up and did not fight anymore. Expect   Not Expect

2. Mr. Jenson complained that his son made a **hash** of maintaining the lawn. He decided to hire a landscape company to help get it back in shape. Expect   Not Expect

3. Santiago liked to watch his mother make dinner. His favorite was watching her make **hash** by mixing chopped meat and potatoes. Expect   Not Expect

4. The young girl was learning to make different types of fruit salad. The most challenging part was making **hash** using oranges and marshmallows. Expect   Not Expect

5. George's parents were proud of the job he had done on his history test. They said he made a **hash** of it. Expect   Not Expect

6. Savannah was very shy around others. She liked to **hash** it out with people at parties and dances. Expect   Not Expect

7. Carly liked whole tomatoes in her salad. She asked her mother to **hash** the tomatoes when she made the salad. Expect   Not Expect

8. The cook used a sharp knife to **hash** the meat. Expect   Not Expect

Create Stories

On a sheet of paper, write a short story or scenario for each of the four meanings of **hash**.

 Pre-Lesson Activity—Meanings of Related Words

1 One meaning of **head** includes the following related words.

a. The **director** can mean a <u>leader</u> of a group of people. For example, "Aaron was the **director** of the school band."

Write a sentence using **director**.

_____

_____

b. A **principal** can mean the <u>leader</u> of a school. For example, "Dr. Rice is the **principal** of Dawson Creek Elementary School."

Write a sentence using **principal**.

_____

_____

c. **Chief** can mean the <u>leader</u> of an Indian nation. For example, "The **chief** of the tribe decided when the warriors should hunt for buffalo."

Write a sentence using **chief**.

_____

_____

2 A second meaning of **head** includes the following related words.

a. The **peak** means the very <u>top of something</u>. For example, "The **peak** of the rocket ship was the capsule where the astronauts sat."

Write a sentence using **peak**.

_____

_____

b. **Summit** means the <u>top of something</u> or the highest point of a place. For example, "Shannon climbed to the **summit** of the mountain where she could see in every direction."

Write a sentence using **summit**.

_____

_____

c. A **tip** can mean the <u>top of something</u>. For example, "The cat was sitting on the **tip** of the pole."

Write a sentence using **tip**.

_____

_____

3 A third meaning of **head** includes the following related words.

a. An **understanding** can mean having the <u>mental ability</u> to do something. For example, "Although Neal never played football before he had a good **understanding** of the game."

Write a sentence using **understanding**.

_____

_____

b. **Aptitude** can mean having the <u>mental ability</u> to perform a task. For example, "Keri had a strong **aptitude** for music and could play almost any song she heard on the radio with her guitar."

Write a sentence using **aptitude**.

_____

_____

c. **Capacity** can mean having the <u>mental ability</u> to complete an assignment. For example, "Since Howard was too young for school, he did not have the **capacity** to understand his older brother's math homework."

Write a sentence using **capacity**.

_____

_____

4 A fourth meaning of **head** has no related words.

a. When **head** is used in this way, it means the <u>part of the body containing your eyes, mouth, nose, and brain</u>. For example, "Jodie hit the soccer ball with her **head** to score the winning goal."

Write a sentence using **head**.

_____

_____

Word Meaning in Context

Head began in the Old German language as a word meaning "a bowl or skull." Later, in the English language, this meaning expanded to include four current meanings:

- ❏ **leader**
- ❏ **top of something**
- ❏ **mental ability**
- ❏ **part of body containing your eyes, mouth, nose, and brain**

1. Wearing a helmet while mountain biking can prevent **head** injuries.

Which of the meanings of **head** is this? _____

_____

2. Mr. Gonzales is the **head** of the company and is in charge of all the employees.

Which of the meanings of **head** is this? _____

_____

3. Rhonda grabbed the **head** of the pin to make sure she didn't accidentally poke herself while sewing.

Which of the meanings of **head** is this? _____

_____

4. The football coach thought his quarterback Cody had a good **head** for the game.

Which of the meanings of **head** is this? _____

_____

Word Meaning Map   The teacher will give you the **Head** worksheet.

Complete Each Definition

1. A **head** can be a person who is the _____ of a group of people.

2. **Head** can also mean the _____ of something.

3. **Head** can also mean that a person has the _____ ability to perform a certain task.

4. **Head** can also mean the part of your _____ containing your eyes, mouth, nose, and brain.

Understanding Check

Circle whether **head** is used as you would expect.

1. Freddy was 14 and got his very first job delivering newspapers. He couldn't wait to tell his parents about his new job as **head** of the newspaper.   Expect   Not Expect

2. Shelby loved to climb mountains and would always camp at the **head** of one. Last weekend, she did as she usually did and camped at the base or bottom of the mountain.   Expect   Not Expect

3. Chaz formed his own musical band so he could sing and write all of his own songs. He really wanted to be the **head** of his own band.   Expect   Not Expect

4. Dawn lived with her family on the top floor of the apartment building. Her apartment was the first door on the right once you reached the **head** of the staircase.   Expect   Not Expect

5. Marsha plays basketball and has twisted her ankle several times while playing. To protect her **head** she has begun to wear an ankle brace.   Expect   Not Expect

6. Ivy loved taking math courses. Her parents and teachers always said she had a good **head** for math.   Expect   Not Expect

7. Jill never played sports while in school. She felt she had developed a good **head** for sports due to her lack of participation.   Expect   Not Expect

8. Deon really likes riding his motorcycle with his friends. He always makes sure to wear a helmet to protect his **head** in the case of an accident.   Expect   Not Expect

Create Stories

On a sheet of paper, write a short story or scenario for each of the four meanings of **head**.

 Pre-Lesson Activity—Meanings of Related Words

1 One meaning of **heel** includes the following related words.

a. **Butt** can mean the <u>back part of a foot, shoe, or palm</u>. For example, "In karate class, Lila learned how to strike her opponent with the **butt** of her hand."

Write a sentence using **butt**.

_____

_____

b. **Tail end** can mean the <u>back part of a foot, shoe, or palm</u>. For example, "Bernice caught the **tail end** of her foot in the car door."

Write a sentence using **tail end**.

_____

_____

c. **Backside** can mean the <u>back part of a foot, shoe, or palm</u>. For example, "Tommy knew he needed new sneakers once the **backside** of his tennis shoes wore out."

Write a sentence using **backside**.

_____

_____

2 A second meaning of **heel** includes the following related words.

a. **Scoundrel** means a <u>person who is disgraceful</u>. For example, "The con man was a **scoundrel** who cheated innocent people out of their money."

Write a sentence using **scoundrel**.

_____

_____

b. **Cad** means a <u>person who is disgraceful</u>. For example, "The villain in the cartoon was a **cad** who lied to everyone he met."

Write a sentence using **cad**.

_____

_____

c. **Swine** can mean a <u>person who is disgraceful</u>. For example, "The person who vandalized the church was a **swine**."

Write a sentence using **swine**.

_____

_____

3 A third meaning of **heel** has no related words.

a. When **heel** is used in this way, it means the <u>lower end of a mast or boom</u>. For example, "The **heel** of the sailboat's mast was made from oak so it would be strong enough to withstand heavy winds."

Write a sentence using **heel**.

_____

_____

4 A fourth meaning of **heel** has no related words.

a. When **heel** is used in this way, it means a <u>position close behind</u>. For example, "At obedience school John practiced making his puppy **heel** on a leash."

Write a sentence using **heel**.

_____

_____

Word Meaning in Context

Heel began in the Old English language as a word meaning "conceal." Later, this meaning expanded to include four current meanings:

- ❏ **back part of a foot, shoe, or palm**
- ❏ **person who is disgraceful**
- ❏ **lower end of a mast or boom**
- ❏ **position close behind**

1. Nobody wanted to bring Jim's Great Dane for a walk because he had never learned to **heel** and would constantly pull when on a leash.

Which of the meanings of **heel** is this? _____

_____

2. Janice was limping after she bruised the **heel** of her foot.

Which of the meanings of **heel** is this? _____

_____

3. My sister's last boyfriend was such a **heel** that he never even offered to drive her home after a date.

Which of the meanings of **heel** is this? _____

_____

4. When the sailboat turned into the wind, the **heel** of the boom swung across the deck and hit the sailor on the head.

Which of the meanings of **heel** is this? _____

_____

Word Meaning Map   The teacher will give you the **Heel** worksheet.

Complete Each Definition

1. Heel can mean the _____ part of a foot, shoe, or palm.

2. Heel can also mean a person who is _____ .

3. Heel can also mean the lower end of a mast or _____ on a sailboat.

4. Heel can also mean a position close _____ .

✓ Understanding Check

Circle whether **heel** is used as you would expect.

1. Wayne's sailboat was damaged during the storm. He spent the weekend repairing the mast's **heel**.　　Expect　　Not Expect

2. Susan's older brother was very protective of her. He would never let her go out with a boy unless he was a **heel**.　　Expect　　Not Expect

3. The animals at the dog show were very well behaved. All of the dogs would **heel** by their masters' sides.　　Expect　　Not Expect

4. Last night Brian walked into the bathroom door by accident and stubbed his big toe. He said his **heel** hurt all night.　　Expect　　Not Expect

5. Elizabeth never liked to wear new shoes. She said it usually took several weeks before the shoes were broken in enough to be comfortable around the **heel**.　　Expect　　Not Expect

6. Tonya took sailing lessons over the summer. Her favorite part of sailing was using the **heel** to steer the boat.　　Expect　　Not Expect

7. Most cats do not like to be walked on a leash. Almost all cats will naturally **heel** once they are put on a leash, making it very difficult to walk.　　Expect　　Not Expect

8. The mechanic began to charge customers for repairs he never made. When customers realized that he was a **heel**, they stopped doing business with him.　　Expect　　Not Expect

Create Stories

On a sheet of paper, write a short story or scenario for each of the four meanings of **heel**.

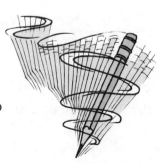

The Multiple Meaning Vocabulary Program

Height

Pre-Lesson Activity—Meanings of Related Words

1 One meaning of **height** includes the following related words.

   a. **Altitude** means the <u>distance above the ground</u>. For example, "The plane was flying in the jet stream at a very high **altitude**."

   Write a sentence using **altitude**.

_____

_____

   b. **Elevation** can mean the <u>distance above the ground</u>. For example, "The chairlift brought the skiers up the mountain to a very high **elevation**."

   Write a sentence using **elevation**.

_____

_____

2 A second meaning of **height** includes the following related words.

   a. **Peak** can mean when something is <u>at its most successful point</u>. For example, "The Denver Broncos were at their **peak** when they won the Super Bowl."

   Write a sentence using **peak**.

_____

_____

   b. **Prime** can mean when something is <u>at its most successful point</u>. For example, "When skateboarding was in its **prime**, most kids were hoping to get a new board for Christmas."

   Write a sentence using **prime**.

_____

_____

c. **Heyday** can mean something <u>at its most successful point</u>. For example, "Muhammad Ali's **heyday** was when he reigned as the heavyweight boxing championship of the world."

Write a sentence using **heyday**.

_____

_____

3 A third meaning of **height** includes the following related words.

a. **Hilltop** can mean a <u>high place</u> above a hill. For example, "Selina thought the view from the **hilltop** was breathtaking."

Write a sentence using **hilltop**.

_____

_____

b. **Bluff** can mean a <u>high place</u> above a hill. For example, "Toby's house sat on the **bluff** overlooking the prairie."

Write a sentence using **bluff**.

_____

_____

c. **Knoll** can mean a <u>high place</u> above a hill. For example, "The gnome lived on the **knoll** inside a big oak tree."

Write a sentence using **knoll**.

_____

_____

Word Meaning in Context

Height began in the Old German language as a word meaning "condition of being high." Later, in the English language, this meaning expanded to include three current meanings:

- ❏ **distance above the ground**
- ❏ **at its most successful point**
- ❏ **high place**

1. The lighthouse sat on the **height** so ships could see it for miles in the darkness.

Which of the meanings of **height** is this?_____

_____

2. The little boy was amazed at the **height** of the basketball players when he went to see a professional basketball game with his uncle.

Which of the meanings of **height** is this?_____

_____

3. The Backstreet Boys were at the **height** of their musical career a few years ago.

Which of the meanings of **height** is this?_____

_____

Word Meaning Map   The teacher will give you the **Height** worksheet.

Complete Each Definition

1. **Height** can mean the _____ something is above the ground.

2. **Height** can also mean being at its most _____ point.

3. **Height** can also mean a high _____ such as a hill.

Understanding Check

Circle whether **height** is used as you would expect.

1. The basketball coach assigned the player with the most **height** to play center on the team. He was taller than anyone else.   Expect   Not Expect

2. We loved to watched Michael Jordan play basketball for the Chicago Bulls. He was a truly amazing player and was at the **height** of his basketball career.   Expect   Not Expect

3. The farm was built on the lowest point of the valley where the soil was rich for farming. The farm was built on the **height** overlooking the town.   Expect   Not Expect

4. Elizabeth stared at the mansion built on the **height** and wondered what type of views it would have of the town below.   Expect   Not Expect

5. Britney Spears was at the **height** of her career in elementary school before she started singing.   Expect   Not Expect

6. Daniel put the tape measure around his waist to measure his **height**.   Expect   Not Expect

Create Stories

On a sheet of paper, write a short story or scenario for each of the three meanings of **height**.

 **Hide**

 Pre-Lesson Activity—Meanings of Related Words

1 One meaning of **hide** includes the following related words.

    a. **Conceal** can mean to <u>prevent from being seen</u>. For example, "John tried to **conceal** his black eye from his mother when he got home from school."
Write a sentence using **conceal**.

_____

_____

    b. **Cover** can mean to <u>prevent from being seen</u>. For example, "Sandy put a magazine over her letter to **cover** it so others couldn't read it when she left the room."
Write a sentence using **cover**.

_____

_____

    c. **Obscure** can mean to <u>prevent from being seen</u>. For example, "The army used smoke to **obscure** the movement of soldiers on the battlefield."
Write a sentence using **obscure**.

_____

_____

2 A second meaning of **hide** includes the following related words.

    a. **Keep secret** means <u>to conceal from knowledge</u>. For example, "The spy wanted to **keep secret** all he knew when he was caught by the FBI."
Write a sentence using **keep secret**.

_____

_____

    b. **Keep tight-lipped** can mean <u>to conceal from knowledge</u>. For example, "Diane warned her little sister to **keep tight-lipped** what she knew about her brother's surprise birthday party on Saturday."
Write a sentence using **keep tight-lipped**.

_____

_____

c. **Keep mum** can mean <u>to conceal from knowledge</u>. For example, "Her best friend asked her to **keep mum** about why she was late to school."
Write a sentence using **keep mum**.

_____

_____

3 A third meaning of **hide** includes the following related words.

a. A **hideout** can mean <u>a place built to look like its surroundings</u>. For example, "Bonnie and Clyde used to use a **hideout** after the bank robbery."
Write a sentence using **hideout**.

_____

_____

b. **Hideaway** can mean <u>a place built to look like its surroundings</u>. For example, "The lake cabin was a little **hideaway** that was difficult to see until you came to it."
Write a sentence using **hideaway**.

_____

_____

c. A **blind** can mean <u>a place built to look like its surroundings</u>. For example, "The nature photographer was sitting in a **blind** to take close-up photographs of the birds."
Write a sentence using **blind**.

_____

_____

4 A fourth meaning of **hide** includes the following related words.

a. A **pelt** means the <u>skin of an animal</u>. For example, "The settler wanted to trade a rabbit **pelt** and other goods with the local Indian tribe." Write a sentence using **pelt**.

_____

_____

b. A **coat** can mean the <u>skin of an animal</u>. For example, "Jill thought the otter's **coat** was very shiny and soft to the touch."
Write a sentence using **coat**.

_____

_____

c. **Fur** can mean the <u>skin of an animal</u>. For example, "The rabbit's **fur** matched the grass, allowing him to avoid being eaten by other animals."
Write a sentence using **fur**.

_____

_____

Word Meaning in Context

Hide began in the Old English language as a word meaning "conceal." Later, this meaning expanded to include four current meanings:

- ❏ **prevent from being seen**
- ❏ **conceal from knowledge**
- ❏ **place built to look like its surroundings**
- ❏ **the skin of an animal**

1. Early pioneers used the **hide** from animals to make their clothes.

Which of the meanings of **hide** is this?_____

_____

2. Every Easter my mom would **hide** candy around the house.

Which of the meanings of **hide** is this?_____

_____

3. Ivan tried to **hide** his school detention from his mother.

Which of the meanings of **hide** is this?_____

_____

4. The man spent most of the day building a **hide** that he would use during hunting season.

Which of the meanings of **hide** is this?_____

_____

Word Meaning Map   The teacher will give you the **Hide** worksheet.

Complete Each Definition

1. **Hide** can mean to prevent from being _____.

2. **Hide** can also mean to _____ from knowledge.

3. **Hide** can also mean a place built to look _____ its surroundings.

4. **Hide** can also mean the _____ of an animal.

Understanding Check

Circle whether **hide** is used as you would expect.

1. Tim was crouching behind a bush in the backyard. He was playing a game of **hide** and seek with his best friend.   Expect   Not Expect

2. Troy was telling everyone he knew about the A+ he received on his science test. He was trying to **hide** how well he did.   Expect   Not Expect

3. The hunter wanted to make sure the ducks wouldn't be able to see him when they flew overhead. While it was still dark, he climbed into a **hide** by the lake.   Expect   Not Expect

4. Susan thought it was cruel to use animals for clothing or food. She made sure all of her clothing was made from **hide** since she didn't want to hurt any animals.   Expect   Not Expect

5. Larry really wanted to meet the new girl in school. Every time he saw her in the hallway, he made sure to **hide** so he would have a chance to say hello.   Expect   Not Expect

6. Karen told her best friend that she had a crush on her neighbor. She didn't want anyone to know, though, and made her friend promise to **hide** the truth.   Expect   Not Expect

7. The lost hiker was hoping to be spotted by the airplane. He thought it would be best to stay in the open area in a **hide** so he could be easily seen.   Expect   Not Expect

8. The leather shop would make just about any type of clothing a customer wanted. Jason found a **hide** he liked and asked if they could make a purse from it for his mother.   Expect   Not Expect

Create Stories

On a sheet of paper, write a short story or scenario for each of the four meanings of **hide**.

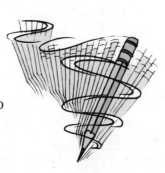

Huddle

Pre-Lesson Activity—Meanings of Related Words

1 One meaning of **huddle** includes the following related words.

a. **Snuggle** can mean to <u>curl one's limbs close to the body</u>. For example, "When babies get cold they **snuggle** up tight to keep warm."

Write a sentence using **snuggle**.

_____

_____

b. **Nestle** can mean to <u>curl one's limbs close to the body</u>. For example, "After the dog came in from the cold, he would **nestle** up by the fire to warm up."

Write a sentence using **nestle**.

_____

_____

c. **Cuddle** can mean to <u>curl one's limbs close to the body</u>. For example, "A mother may **cuddle** with her children when they are reading a book."

Write a sentence using **cuddle**.

_____

_____

2 A second meaning of **huddle** includes the following related words.

a. **Cluster** can mean to <u>crowd together</u>. For example, "The people had to **cluster** in a small area outside the theater before they opened the doors."

Write a sentence using **cluster**.

_____

_____

b. **Group** can mean to <u>crowd together</u>. For example, "The principal wanted to **group** students together by grades in the auditorium."

Write a sentence using **group**.

_____

_____

c. **Bunch** can mean to <u>crowd together</u>. For example, "On New Year's Eve, thousands of people would **bunch** together in the city square waiting for midnight."

Write a sentence using **bunch**.

_____

_____

3 A third meaning of **huddle** includes the following related words.

a. **Discussion** can mean a <u>small private conference</u>. For example, "The pitcher and catcher had a **discussion** on the mound before the baseball game started."

Write a sentence using **discussion**.

_____

_____

b. **Powwow** can mean a <u>small private conference</u>. For example, "Sandy would have a **powwow** with her parents every time they had a disagreement."

Write a sentence using **powwow**.

_____

_____

c. **Confer** can mean a <u>small private conference</u>. For example, "Sean's parents wanted to **confer** with his teacher after he started doing poorly in math."

Write a sentence using **confer**.

_____

_____

Word Meaning in Context

Huddle began in the Old English language as a word meaning "to hide."
Later, this meaning expanded to include three current meanings:

- ❏ **curl one's limbs close to the body**
- ❏ **crowd together**
- ❏ **small private conference**

1. The principal came into the classroom for a moment to **huddle** with the teacher about something.

Which of the meanings of **huddle** is this? _____

_____

2. The Boy Scouts were told to **huddle** in their sleeping bags if they got cold during the night.

Which of the meanings of **huddle** is this? _____

_____

3. The coach told all the players to **huddle** together so he wouldn't have to yell.

Which of the meanings of **huddle** is this? _____

_____

Word Meaning Map   The teacher will give you the **Huddle** worksheet.

Complete Each Definition

1. **Huddle** can mean to _____
one's limbs close to the body.

2. **Huddle** can also mean to _____ together.

3. **Huddle** can also mean a small _____ conference.

Understanding Check

Circle whether **huddle** is used as you would expect.

1. The entire school had to **huddle** into the theater for the assembly. After everyone was seated, the principal announced the guest speaker.

   Expect   Not Expect

2. Charlie's parents wanted to have a **huddle** to discuss if they should let him go to a friend's party on Saturday night. They asked Charlie to meet them in the living room after dinner.

   Expect   Not Expect

3. Sally was the only person on the bus, so she had to **huddle** in the back. She sat quietly and read her book on the bus.

   Expect   Not Expect

4. When Bridgette got too hot at night, she would **huddle** under her warm blankets. She often did this on hot summer nights.

   Expect   Not Expect

5. Drake's mom knew he was getting cold when he got out of the pool to **huddle** under his towel. The sun was not shining and the wind was blowing.

   Expect   Not Expect

6. Jenny's dad told her he wanted to have a **huddle** with her about getting a new bike. He sent her to her room and did not discuss anything.

   Expect   Not Expect

Create Stories

On a sheet of paper, write a short story or scenario for each of the three meanings of **huddle**.

Innocent

Pre-Lesson Activity—Meanings of Related Words

1   One meaning of **innocent** includes the following related words.

a. **Blameless** can mean <u>not guilty of an offense</u>. For example, "The police officer said the young driver was **blameless** and was not responsible for the car accident."

Write a sentence using **blameless**.

_____

_____

b. **Guiltless** can mean <u>not guilty of an offense</u>. For example, "The boy told his mother that he was **guiltless** and didn't break the lamp in the living room."

Write a sentence using **guiltless**.

_____

_____

c. **In the clear** can mean <u>not guilty of an offense</u>. For example, "The teacher told Kyle that he was **in the clear** of being tardy because he brought a note from his mother."

Write a sentence using **in the clear**.

_____

_____

2   A second meaning of **innocent** includes the following related words.

a. **Naive** can mean <u>not experienced</u>. For example, "The seniors thought the incoming freshmen were very **naive**."

Write a sentence using **naive**.

_____

_____

b. **Unsophisticated** can mean <u>not experienced</u>. For example, "Everyone thought Janice was **unsophisticated** when she showed up at the formal dance wearing jeans."

Write a sentence using **unsophisticated**.

_____

_____

c. **Unaware** can mean <u>not experienced</u>. For example, "The school bully liked to pick on new students because they were usually **unaware** and more likely to fall for his pranks."

Write a sentence using **unaware**.

_____

_____

3 A third meaning of **innocent** includes the following related words.

a. **Harmless** can mean <u>not dangerous or harmful</u>. For example, "Diane pulled a **harmless** prank on her sister as an April Fool's joke."

Write a sentence using **harmless**.

_____

_____

b. **Risk free** can mean <u>not dangerous or harmful</u>. For example, "Even though the trip was **risk free**, Bill and Tara said they would never take a float trip down the river again."

Write a sentence using **risk free**.

_____

_____

c. **Playful** can mean <u>not dangerous or harmful</u>. For example, "The tiny lion cubs fought with each other in a **playful** manner."

Write a sentence using **playful**.

_____

_____

Word Meaning in Context

Innocent began in the Old French language as a word meaning "harmless." Later, in the English language, this meaning expanded to include three current meanings:

❏ **not guilty of an offense**

❏ **not experienced**

❏ **not dangerous or harmful**

1. Julie thought she was making an **innocent** comment about her friend's new hairstyle, but her friend became very upset.

Which of the meanings of **innocent** is this? _____

_____

2. The jury found the defendant **innocent** on all charges.

Which of the meanings of **innocent** is this? _____

_____

3. The experienced football players all thought the new rookie was too **innocent** to play in a Super Bowl game.

Which of the meanings of **innocent** is this? _____

_____

Word Meaning Map   The teacher will give you the **Innocent** worksheet.

Complete Each Definition

1. Innocent can mean not _____
of an offense or wrongdoing.

2. Innocent can also mean not _____ or harmful.

3. Innocent can also mean not _____ .

Understanding Check

Circle whether **innocent** is used as you would expect.

1. The criminal confessed to the crime at the scene. Dozens of
    witnesses saw him commit the robbery, so everyone knew
    he was **innocent**.   Expect   Not Expect

2. The two older men were sitting on the park bench and were
    talking about the weather. Their conversation was **innocent**
    and friendly.   Expect   Not Expect

3. Brad was the student body president and knew most of the
    students in the school. Anyone who wanted to find out
    about what was going on at school usually came to him
    because he was so **innocent**.   Expect   Not Expect

4. Alex was very upset with his little brother. He started to
    make **innocent** comments about him to make him upset
    and cry.   Expect   Not Expect

5. Roberto's mother saw him playing with his friends outside
    when the glass bowl was broken. Knowing he was **innocent**,
    she began to ask his sister about what happened instead.   Expect   Not Expect

6. Debra never liked to swear because she thought it was rude.
    Some of her classmates thought they could trick her into
    swearing by saying she was too **innocent** to know
    such words.   Expect   Not Expect

Create Stories

On a sheet of paper, write a short story or scenario
for each of the three meanings of **innocent**.

Instrument

Pre-Lesson Activity—Meanings of Related Words

1 One meaning of **instrument** includes the following related words.

   a. **Channel** can mean the <u>method by which something is achieved</u>. For example, "The owner of the company believed the **channel** to his succcess was that he always tried to keep his customers happy."

       Write a sentence using **channel**.

       _____

       _____

   b. **Vehicle** can mean the <u>method by which something is achieved</u>. For example, "Diana thought that maintaining good grades in school was the **vehicle** for getting into the college of her choice."

       Write a sentence using **vehicle**.

       _____

       _____

   c. **Factor** can mean the <u>method by which something is achieved</u>. For example, "The police told the press that the eyewitness was the main **factor** that allowed them to catch the thief."

       Write a sentence using **factor**.

       _____

       _____

2 A second meaning of **instrument** includes the following related words.

   a. **Tool** can mean a <u>utensil or implement</u>. For example, "The dentist was using a small **tool** called a pick to help find cavities in the patient's mouth."

       Write a sentence using **tool**.

       _____

       _____

b. **Mechanism** can mean a <u>utensil or implement</u>. For example, "The surgeon showed the patient a small **mechanism** that would be used during the operation."

Write a sentence using **mechanism**.

_____

_____

c. **Gadget** can mean a <u>utensil or implement</u>. For example, "Anna bought her mom a **gadget** she saw on TV that promised to save her time and money when cleaning the house."

Write a sentence using **gadget**.

_____

_____

3 A third meaning of **instrument** has no related words.

a. When **instrument** is used in this way, it means a <u>device used to produce music</u>. For example, "Dominic loved to play his **instrument** in music class."

Write a sentence using **instrument**.

_____

_____

4 A fourth meaning of **instrument** has no related words.

a. When **instrument** is used in this way, it means a <u>device for recording, measuring, or controlling</u>. For example, "The pilot kept scanning the **instrument** panel to make sure the plane was on course."

Write a sentence using **instrument**.

_____

_____

Word Meaning in Context

Instrument began in the prehistoric Indo-European language as a word meaning "power and strength." Later, in the English language, this meaning expanded to include four current meanings:

- ❏ **method by which something is achieved**
- ❏ **utensil or implement**
- ❏ **device used to produce music**
- ❏ **device for recording, measuring, or controlling**

1. The ship's captain asked the navigator to take another **instrument** reading to make sure that they wouldn't accidentally run aground in shallow waters.

Which of the meanings of **instrument** is this?_____

_____

2. The press thought the team's pitching was the **instrument** responsible for getting the Yankees into the World Series.

Which of the meanings of **instrument** is this?_____

_____

3. The jeweler used a special **instrument** to work on the miniature components of the watch.

Which of the meanings of **instrument** is this?_____

_____

4. The conductor was bragging that he could play every **instrument** in the symphony.

Which of the meanings of **instrument** is this?_____

_____

Word Meaning Map   The teacher will give you the **Instrument** worksheet.

Complete Each Definition

1. **Instrument** can mean a method by which something is _____

_____ .

2. **Instrument** can also mean a _____ or implement.

3. **Instrument** can also mean a device used to produce _____ .

4. **Instrument** can also mean a measuring device used for recording, _____ , or controlling.

Understanding Check

Circle whether **instrument** is used as you would expect.

1. Tim was sick during the state soccer finals and played very little during the tournament. The coach said his performance was the **instrument** that allowed them to win the championship. Expect   Not Expect

2. Jason played touch football with his friends every Saturday morning. This Saturday it was his turn to bring the **instrument** to play in the game. Expect   Not Expect

3. During the early days of aviation, planes didn't have much navigation equipment on board. The compass was often the only **instrument** pilots had to help them find an airport. Expect   Not Expect

4. Samantha sold more Girl Scout cookies than anyone in her school. The scout leader told everyone that Samantha was the main **instrument** for the cookie sale's success. Expect   Not Expect

5. There are typically two pilots aboard a passenger aircraft. Both pilots sit on the **instrument** located at the front of the plane. Expect   Not Expect

6. Andrea is going to school to learn how to be a car mechanic. Each day she learns about a different **instrument** she will use to repair cars. Expect   Not Expect

7. Janice went to the symphony and really liked the sound of the violin. When she got home, she asked her parents if she could take music lessons so she could play that **instrument**. Expect   Not Expect

8. The dentist asked the dental assistant to hand him an **instrument** during one of his examinations. She handed him an x-ray showing the patient's teeth. Expect   Not Expect

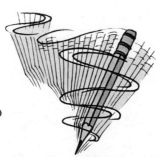

Create Stories

On a sheet of paper, write a short story or scenario for each of the four meanings of **instrument**.

| # Interest

Pre-Lesson Activity—Meanings of Related Words

1 One meaning of **interest** includes the following related words.

a. **Claim** can mean a <u>right or legal share of something</u>. For example, "Bruno was supposed to have a **claim** in his rich uncle's estate."

Write a sentence using **claim**.

_____

_____

b. **Stock** can mean a <u>right or legal share of something</u>. For example, "My grandmother bought me **stock** as an investment to pay for my college."

Write a sentence using **stock**.

_____

_____

c. **Equity** can mean a <u>right or legal share of something</u>. For example, "After building the store together, both friends had shared **equity** in the business."

Write a sentence using **equity**.

_____

_____

2 A second meaning of **interest** includes the following related words.

a. **Percentage** can mean a <u>charge for borrowed money</u>. For example, "Dad wanted to buy a new car now while the **percentage** rate for loans was very low."

Write a sentence using **percentage**.

_____

_____

b. **Points** can mean a <u>charge for borrowed money</u>. For example, "Banks earn money from the **points** they charge on the loans they make."

Write a sentence using **points**.

_____

_____

c. **Return** can mean a <u>charge for borrowed money</u>. For example, "Janice received a high rate of **return** from the money she had in her bank account."

Write a sentence using **return**.

_____

_____

3 A third meaning of **interest** includes the following related words.

a. **Curiosity** can mean a <u>concern about something or someone</u>. For example, "Drew always had a **curiosity** in reading about mummies in Egypt."

Write a sentence using **curiosity**.

_____

_____

b. **Fascination** can mean a <u>concern about something or someone</u>. For example, "Chris has a **fascination** with flying and wants to be a pilot when he grows up."

Write a sentence using **fascination**.

_____

_____

c. **Caringness** can mean a <u>concern about something or someone</u>. For example, "Parents really liked the way that Mrs. Smith showed **caringness** toward the children in her classroom."

Write a sentence using **caringness**.

_____

_____

Word Meaning in Context

Interest began in the Old French language as a word meaning "damage."
Later, in the English language, this meaning expanded and changed
to include three current meanings:

- ❑ **right or legal share in something**
- ❑ **charge for borrowed money**
- ❑ **concern about something or someone**

1. We all have an **interest** in our children's education.

Which of the meanings of **interest** is this? _____

_____

2. Drew's grandfather sold his **interest** in the family business to his children once he retired.

Which of the meanings of **interest** is this? _____

_____

3. When you put money into a bank account, you will earn **interest**.

Which of the meanings of **interest** is this? _____

_____

Word Meaning Map   The teacher will give you the **Interest** worksheet.

Complete Each Definition

1. **Interest** can mean a right or legal _____
in something.

2. **Interest** can also mean a _____ for borrowed money.

3. **Interest** can also mean a _____ about something
or someone.

Understanding Check

Circle whether **interest** is used as you would expect.

1. Johnny always tried to make as much money as he could. He
   even chose his bank based on how much **interest** they paid.   Expect   Not Expect

2. Sandra had never met any of her cousins because they lived
   out of state. She felt as if she had a strong **interest** in
   their lives.   Expect   Not Expect

3. Jill's dad wanted her to take over the family business. When
   she turned 18, he began to give her a larger **interest**
   in the store.   Expect   Not Expect

4. Randy opened up a new bank account yesterday. He deposited
   twenty dollars of **interest** into the account.   Expect   Not Expect

5. Derek's uncle had coached him in baseball since he was six
   years old. As Derek grew up, his uncle's **interest** in his athletic
   abilities increased.   Expect   Not Expect

6. James never played the lottery. When the 100-million-dollar
   jackpot was awarded, he knew he would have an **interest**
   in the winnings.   Expect   Not Expect

Create Stories

On a sheet of paper, write a short story or scenario
for each of the three meanings of **interest**.

Pre-Lesson Activity—Meanings of Related Words

1 One meaning of **jam** includes the following related words.

a. **Cram** can mean to <u>squeeze into a tight space</u>. For example, "Ashlee tried to **cram** all of her dirty clothes into the washing machine."

Write a sentence using **cram**.

_____

_____

b. **Stuff** can mean to <u>squeeze into a tight space</u>. For example, "Kevin crushed his science project when he tried to **stuff** it into his backpack."

Write a sentence using **stuff**.

_____

_____

c. **Wedge** can mean to <u>squeeze into a tight space</u>. For example, "The janitor tried to **wedge** the doorstop underneath the door to keep it open."

Write a sentence using **wedge**.

_____

_____

2 A second meaning of **jam** includes the following related words.

a. **Become stuck** can mean to <u>not work because parts become stuck</u>. For example, "If you place too many sheets of paper into the shredder at once, it will **become stuck**."

Write a sentence using **become stuck**.

_____

_____

b. **Break down** can mean to <u>not work because parts become stuck</u>. For example, "The garbage disposal started to **break down** after my little brother stuffed paper down the sink."

Write a sentence using **break down**.

_____

_____

c. **Seize** can mean to <u>not work because parts become stuck</u>. For example, "Car engines can **seize** if their oil levels are not properly maintained."
Write a sentence using **seize**.

_____

_____

3 A third meaning of **jam** includes the following related words.

a. **Dilemma** can mean a <u>difficult situation</u>. For example, "Brenda's **dilemma** was whether she should stay home and study for her math test or go to a friend's party."
Write a sentence using **dilemma**.

_____

_____

b. **Bind** can mean a <u>difficult situation</u>. For example, "Mike was in a **bind** because his bike was broken, but he still had to deliver papers for his newspaper route."
Write a sentence using **bind**.

_____

_____

c. **Predicament** can mean a <u>difficult situation</u>. For example, "Dave's **predicament** was that he didn't have enough money to buy his mom a present for her birthday."
Write a sentence using **predicament**.

_____

_____

4 A fourth meaning of **jam** includes the following related words.

a. **Jelly** means a <u>sweet spread of fruit and sugar</u>. For example, "My favorite flavor of **jelly** is raspberry." Write a sentence using **jelly**.

_____

_____

b. **Preserves** can mean a <u>sweet spread of fruit and sugar</u>. For example, "My mother took first place at the county fair for her homemade strawberry **preserves**."
Write a sentence using **preserves**.

_____

_____

c. **Marmalade** can mean a <u>sweet spread of fruit and sugar</u>. For example, "Dad loves to eat English muffins with **marmalade** for breakfast every morning."
Write a sentence using **marmalade**.

_____

_____

Word Meaning in Context

Jam began in the Old English language as a word meaning "push tightly together." Later, this meaning expanded to include four current meanings:

- ❑ **squeeze into a tight space**
- ❑ **not work because parts become stuck**
- ❑ **difficult situation**
- ❑ **sweet spread of fruit and sugar**

1. John's favorite sandwich was peanut butter and strawberry **jam**.

Which of the meanings of **jam** is this? _____

_____

2. The crowd tried to **jam** into the small theater.

Which of the meanings of **jam** is this? _____

_____

3. The computer keyboard was very old and would **jam** every now and then.

Which of the meanings of **jam** is this? _____

_____

4. Donna tried to lie to her parents when she got herself into a **jam**.

Which of the meanings of **jam** is this? _____

_____

Word Meaning Map   The teacher will give you the **Jam** worksheet.

Complete Each Definition

1. Jam can mean to _____ or force into a tight or confined space.

2. Jam can also mean to not work because parts become _____.

3. Jam can also mean a difficult _____.

4. Jam can also mean a sweet _____ of fruit and sugar.

✓ Understanding Check

Circle whether **jam** is used as you would expect.

1. Susan didn't realize that she promised to go to the dance with two different boys. Her girlfriends laughed at the **jam** she had gotten herself into.　　　　Expect　　　Not Expect

2. Brian was always very lucky. Yesterday he got into a **jam** when he won the school lottery and got free lunches for a week.　　　　Expect　　　Not Expect

3. Jimmy just got a job packing groceries at the market. His boss told him to make sure he didn't **jam** eggs or bread into the bags.　　　　Expect　　　Not Expect

4. Brent was learning how to cook. The first dinner he made was a **jam** made from spaghetti and meatballs.　　　　Expect　　　Not Expect

5. Tim was making fruit smoothies with the blender. The blender began to **jam** after he put in too much ice.　　　　Expect　　　Not Expect

6. Candice moved into her big sister's room after she left for college. Her new room was twice as big, so she needed to **jam** the few things she had into it.　　　　Expect　　　Not Expect

7. Cheryl loved to eat after school. Her favorite snack was **jam** and crackers.　　　　Expect　　　Not Expect

8. Andrea took shop class to learn how to fix household items. After her first class, she knew how to **jam** trash compactors.　　　　Expect　　　Not Expect

Create Stories

On a sheet of paper, write a short story or scenario for each of the four meanings of **jam**.

Joker

Pre-Lesson Activity—Meanings of Related Words

1 One meaning of **joker** includes the following related words.

a. **Prankster** can mean a <u>person who enjoys telling or playing jokes</u>. For example, "Maria is a real **prankster**, which usually makes her a lot of fun to hang out with."

Write a sentence using **prankster**.

_____

_____

b. **Trickster** can mean a <u>person who enjoys telling or playing jokes</u>. For example, "April Fool's Day brings out a little bit of the **trickster** in everyone."

Write a sentence using **trickster**.

_____

_____

c. **Comedian** can mean a <u>person who enjoys telling or playing jokes</u>. For example, "The teacher warned Steven that he was becoming too much of a **comedian** during class."

Write a sentence using **comedian**.

_____

_____

2 A second meaning of **joker** includes the following related words.

a. **Clause** can mean a <u>statement in a contract that changes the meaning</u>. For example, "There is a **clause** in most rental car agreements that changes the definition of an adult driver to someone who is at least 25 years of age."

Write a sentence using **clause**.

_____

_____

b. **Provision** can mean a <u>statement in a contract that changes the meaning</u>. For example, "There is a **provision** in my car loan that states if I am late with a car payment, the interest rate I'm charged may increase."

Write a sentence using **provision**.

_____

_____

c. **Stipulation** can mean a <u>statement in a contract that changes the meaning</u>. For example, "Many products now have a **stipulation** that states a warranty is no longer valid if a product is resold."

Write a sentence using **stipulation**.

_____

_____

3 A third meaning of **joker** has no related words.

a. When **joker** is used in this way, it means a <u>playing card with a picture of a jester</u>. For example, "A lot of card games use the **joker** as a wild card."

Write a sentence using **joker**.

_____

_____

Word Meaning in Context

Joker began in the Old French language as a word meaning "fun and humor." Later, in the English language, the meanings expanded to include three current meanings:

- ❑ **person who enjoys telling or playing jokes**
- ❑ **statement in a contract that changes the meaning**
- ❑ **playing card with a picture of a jester**

1. Before playing solitaire, it is important to remove all of the **jokers** from the deck of cards.

Which of the meanings of **joker** is this? _____

_____

2. The comedic actor was known for being a **joker** when he was growing up.

Which of the meanings of **joker** is this? _____

_____

3. There is a **joker** in my music club agreement that states if I am late with a payment, all future purchases need to be made by credit card.

Which of the meanings of **joker** is this? _____

_____

Word Meaning Map   The teacher will give you the **Joker** worksheet.

Complete Each Definition

1. **Joker** can mean a person who enjoys telling or playing _____
_____ on people.

2. **Joker** can also mean a statement in a contract that _____
the meaning.

3. **Joker** can also mean a playing _____ with a picture
of a jester.

✓ Understanding Check

Circle whether **joker** is used as you would expect.

1. Rich just bought a new deck of playing cards. After opening the deck, the first card he saw was the **joker**.   Expect   Not Expect

2. Terry was a very serious person who rarely found anything funny. She was always known for being quite the **joker**.   Expect   Not Expect

3. Doug could not buy a motorcycle on his own. The motorcycle dealer's sales agreement had a **joker** stating that any customer under 21 years of age is considered a minor and must be accompanied by an adult.   Expect   Not Expect

4. While playing poker with his friends, Chris accidentally turned over one of his cards, showing a big red heart. After that, everyone playing knew he had the **joker**.   Expect   Not Expect

5. Brian was always checking out books on humor from the library. His parents thought that he was a big **joker** who wanted to go into show business when he grew up.   Expect   Not Expect

6. Tim just bought a new stereo from a music store. After he paid the salesman for the stereo, he was given a **joker** that showed the type of stereo he purchased and the price.   Expect   Not Expect

Create Stories

On a sheet of paper, write a short story or scenario for each of the three meanings of **joker**.

Judge

 Pre-Lesson Activity—Meanings of Related Words

1 One meaning of **judge** includes the following related words.

   a. **Magistrate** can mean a <u>person who decides questions in a court of law</u>. For example, "The **magistrate** asked the defendant if he was guilty of the crime of which he was accused."

   Write a sentence using **magistrate**.

   _____

   _____

   b. **Arbitrator** can mean a <u>person who decides questions in a court of law</u>. For example, "When companies have a disagreement on a business contract, they sometimes ask an **arbitrator** to resolve their dispute."

   Write a sentence using **arbitrator**.

   _____

   _____

   c. **Justice** can mean a <u>person who decides questions in a court of law</u>. For example, "After the lawyers kept arguing in the courtroom, the **justice** asked to see them both in her chambers."

   Write a sentence using **justice**.

   _____

   _____

2 A second meaning of **judge** includes the following related words.

   a. **Determine** can mean to <u>form an opinion</u>. For example, "Only after hearing a student's full story could the principal **determine** if it was true or not."

   Write a sentence using **determine**.

   _____

   _____

b. **Conclude** can mean to <u>form an opinion</u>. For example, "The policeman wanted to hear both drivers' accounts of the accident before he would **conclude** who was at fault."

Write a sentence using **conclude**.

_____

_____

c. **Decide** can mean to <u>form an opinion</u>. For example, "After only one class, it was still too early for the students to **decide** if they liked their new art teacher yet."

Write a sentence using **decide**.

_____

_____

3 A third meaning of **judge** includes the following related words.

a. **Referee** can mean a <u>person who decides winners in a competition</u>. For example, "The **referee** in a boxing match should stop the fight anytime one of the fighters can no longer defend himself."

Write a sentence using **referee**.

_____

_____

b. **Umpire** can mean a <u>person who decides winners in a competition</u>. For example, "The **umpire** called the runner who slid into home plate safe."

Write a sentence using **umpire**.

_____

_____

c. **Official** can mean a <u>person who decides winners in a competition</u>. For example, "The football coach asked an **official** to review the instant replay to determine if the receiver caught the football in bounds."

Write a sentence using **official**.

_____

_____

Word Meaning in Context

Judge began in the Old French language as a word meaning "someone who speaks the law." Later, in the English language, this meaning expanded to include three current meanings:

- ❑ **person who decides questions in a court of law**
- ❑ **form an opinion**
- ❑ **person who decides winners in a competition**

1. The finish of the 100-meter dash was so close that the **judge** had a difficult time deciding who came in first.

Which of the meanings of **judge** is this?_____

_____

2. Many young law students hope that some day they will be a **judge** who decides important criminal cases.

Which of the meanings of **judge** is this?_____

_____

3. Veronica hoped her dad wouldn't **judge** her new boyfriend too harshly, because she really liked him.

Which of the meanings of **judge** is this?_____

_____

Word Meaning Map   The teacher will give you the **Judge** worksheet.

Complete Each Definition

1. **Judge** can mean a person who decides questions or cases before a _____

_____ of law.

2. **Judge** can also mean to form an _____ or make an assumption.

3. **Judge** can also mean a person who decides _____ at competitions and sporting events.

Understanding Check

Circle whether **judge** is used as you would expect.

1. Jason didn't study very hard and failed his first science test. He was hoping his teacher wouldn't **judge** his abilities based on that one test and keep him from competing in the school science fair.   Expect   Not Expect

2. The young man was on trial for burglary. He sat in the courtroom next to the **judge** who was supposed to help him during the trial.   Expect   Not Expect

3. Tonya's mother received a speeding ticket last week. Today, she saw the **judge** who determined how much the fine was going to be.   Expect   Not Expect

4. Candice's friends were all talking about a new TV show they watched last night. Candice had not yet seen the program and felt she could accurately **judge** how much she liked the program.   Expect   Not Expect

5. Kyle thought his tennis serve had landed inside the serving box. He complained to the line **judge** who had called the ball out.   Expect   Not Expect

6. Jerissa showed her horse at the annual spring fling horse show. The horse show **judge** was responsible for filling out paperwork so people could participate and did not determine who would win trophies for their efforts.   Expect   Not Expect

Create Stories

On a sheet of paper, write a short story or scenario for each of the three meanings of **judge**.

The Multiple Meaning Vocabulary Program

Pre-Lesson Activity—Meanings of Related Words

1 One meaning of **kid** includes the following related words.

a. **Youth** can mean a <u>child</u> or young person. For example, "Everyone was surprised that the city golf champion was only a **youth**.

Write a sentence using **youth**.

_____

_____

b. **Youngster** can mean a <u>child</u> or young person. For example, "Because Alan was a **youngster**, he could not get in the swimming pool during the adult swim time."

Write a sentence using **youngster**.

_____

_____

c. **Juvenile** can mean a <u>child</u> or young person who is not yet old enough to be considered an adult. For example, "You had to be a **juvenile** to participate in the annual youth chess tournament."

Write a sentence using **juvenile**.

_____

_____

2 A second meaning of **kid** includes the following related words.

a. **Tease** can mean to <u>make a joke</u> or laugh at someone in order to embarrass, annoy, or upset them. For example, "Dominic loved to **tease** Edgar because Dominic was bigger than Edgar was."

Write a sentence using **tease**.

_____

_____

b. **Josh** can mean to <u>make a joke</u> in a gentle and kind way. For example, "Her friends would often **josh** Michaela because of her freckles."

Write a sentence using **josh**.

_____

_____

c. **Banter** can mean to <u>make a joke</u>. For example, "When Chloe and her friends get together they love to be silly and **banter** with one another."

Write a sentence using **banter**.

_____

_____

3 A third meaning of **kid** has no related words.

a. When **kid** is used in this way, it means a <u>young goat or antelope</u>. For example, "The zookeeper made our visit to the zoo very special because he allowed us to pet the goats and the newborn **kid**."

Write a sentence using **kid**.

_____

_____

Word Meaning in Context

Kid began in the Old Scandinavian language as a word meaning "young goat." Later, in the English language, this meaning expanded to include three current meanings:

❑ child

❑ make a joke

❑ young goat or antelope

1. Andriana and her sister Kaylee loved to visit the zoo, where they would pet and feed a mother goat and her **kid**.

   Which of the meanings of **kid** is this? _____

   _____

2. Javier was the only **kid** in his class who had a parrot for a pet.

   Which of the meanings of **kid** is this? _____

   _____

3. Natasha's uncle would always **kid** around when he came to visit.

   Which of the meanings of **kid** is this? _____

   _____

Word Meaning Map   The teacher will give you the **Kid** worksheet.

Complete Each Definition

1. **Kid** can mean a _____ or young person who is not yet old enough to be regarded as an adult.

2. **Kid** can also mean to make a _____ or tease someone.

3. **Kid** can also mean a young _____ or antelope.

Understanding Check

Circle whether **kid** is used as you would expect.

1. The students like to **kid** their teacher because he tells very silly jokes. He is everyone's favorite teacher.

   Expect   Not Expect

2. Krystal plays the cello and the piano. She is an intelligent **kid** who learns very quickly.

   Expect   Not Expect

3. The math teacher was trying to **kid** Omar. She said, "Two plus two equals four."

   Expect   Not Expect

4. One of the goats on the farm where Kylie lived had a **kid**. Kylie named her Daisy.

   Expect   Not Expect

5. Derrick chose books about monkeys. He learned that a grown-up monkey is called a **kid**.

   Expect   Not Expect

6. Jocelyn listed some of the benefits of being a **kid**. These benefits included being able to vote, drive a car, and buy a house.

   Expect   Not Expect

Create Stories

On a sheet of paper, write a short story or scenario for each of the three meanings of **kid**.

 **Knot**

Pre-Lesson Activity—Meanings of Related Words

1 One meaning of **knot** has no related words.

a. When **knot** is used in this way, it means a <u>fastening made by tying together lengths of material</u>. For example, "Frank learned to make a strong **knot** with a rope at camp one summer."

Write a sentence using **knot**.

_____

_____

2 A second meaning of **knot** includes the following related words.

a. **Node** can mean a knob or <u>small hard area on a tree or piece of wood</u>. For example, "The big oak tree in Robin's backyard had a **node** in the trunk."

Write a sentence using **node**.

_____

_____

b. **Gnarl** can mean a bulge or <u>small hard area on a tree or piece of wood</u>. For example, "Collin and Troy used the **gnarl** on the tree as a target and tried to hit it with the football."

Write a sentence using **gnarl**.

_____

_____

c. **Knar** means a lump or <u>small hard area on a tree or piece of wood</u>. For example, "Daisy's favorite tree in her grandmother's backyard had a **knar** in the trunk."

Write a sentence using **knar**.

_____

_____

3 A third meaning of **knot** includes the following related words.

a. **Twinge** can mean a sudden short <u>feeling of tightness in the stomach</u>. For example, "Roberto felt a **twinge** in his stomach when the teacher asked him to give a speech in front of the entire school."

Write a sentence using **twinge**.

_____

_____

b. **Pang** can mean a sudden, sharp <u>feeling of tightness in the stomach</u>. For example, "Except for a small **pang** in his stomach, Jeremiah was feeling much better."

Write a sentence using **pang**.

_____

_____

c. **Cramp** can mean a painful <u>feeling of tightness in the stomach</u>. For example, "After soccer practice Jonathan had a **cramp** in his stomach."

Write a sentence using **cramp**.

_____

_____

4 A fourth meaning of **knot** has no related words.

a. When **knot** is used in this way, it means a <u>unit used for measuring the speed of ships and aircraft</u>. For example, "Dana learned that if a boat was traveling one **knot**, it would travel one nautical mile per hour or approximately 1.85 kilometers per hour."

Write a sentence using **knot**.

_____

_____

Word Meaning in Context

Knot began in the Old German language as a word meaning "round lump." Later, in the English language, this meaning expanded to include four current meanings:

- ❑ **fastening made by tying together lengths of material**
- ❑ **small hard area on a tree or piece of wood**
- ❑ **feeling of tightness in the stomach**
- ❑ **unit used for measuring the speed of ships and aircraft**

1. Philip's boat won the race because it was one **knot** faster than the other boats.

Which of the meanings of **knot** is this? _____

_____

2. Sergio liked to tie his shoestrings in a double **knot**.

Which of the meanings of **knot** is this? _____

_____

3. The saw that Fernando was using to cut some wood buckled when it hit a **knot**.

Which of the meanings of **knot** is this? _____

_____

4. Jillian had a **knot** in her stomach as she ran onto the court for the big volleyball match.

Which of the meanings of **knot** is this? _____

_____

Word Meaning Map   The teacher will give you the **Knot** worksheet.

Complete Each Definition

1. **Knot** can mean a _____ made by tying together lengths of material, such as rope, in a prescribed way.

2. **Knot** can also mean a small hard area on a tree or piece of _____, at a point from which a stem or branch grew.

3. **Knot** can also mean a feeling of _____ in your stomach because you are afraid or excited.

4. **Knot** can also mean a unit used for measuring the _____ of ships and aircraft.

Understanding Check

Circle whether **knot** is used as you would expect.

1. Andre had to tie a very strong **knot** in the rope he used to tie his dog to a tree. He did not want his dog to run into the street.

   Expect   Not Expect

2. Cassidy and her father went to the lumber store for wood. She noticed the round and dark **knot** that was on a piece of lumber that her father bought.

   Expect   Not Expect

3. Johnny's father raced boats for a hobby. His father's speedboat was streamlined to get every possible **knot** of speed out of it.

   Expect   Not Expect

4. Raven's classmates had to share their reports in front of the class. When she heard the teacher say that she would be the next one to give her report in front of the whole class, she felt a **knot** in her stomach.

   Expect   Not Expect

5. Jade and her friend Angel were calm and quiet one afternoon when they were playing a board game at Angel's house. Angel had a **knot** in her stomach.

   Expect   Not Expect

6. Summer made a birthday cake for her mother. She measured one **knot** of sugar and three cups of flour to put in it.

   Expect   Not Expect

7. Alejandra watered a tree in her backyard. It was a perfect tree in every way. It had a large **knot** on one side of it.

   Expect   Not Expect

8. Edwin had two ropes and laid one rope on top of the other. The **knot** was not very strong and came apart easily.

   Expect   Not Expect

Create Stories

On a sheet of paper, write a short story or scenario for each of the four meanings of **knot**.

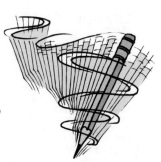

Lace

Pre-Lesson Activity—Meanings of Related Words

1 One meaning of **lace** includes the following related words.

a. **Meshwork** can mean a <u>delicate fabric woven in patterns</u>. For example, "The table cloth at the restaurant had geometric designs sewn into the **meshwork**."

Write a sentence using **meshwork**.

_____

_____

b. **Netting** can mean a <u>delicate fabric woven in patterns</u>. For example, "The bride's veil was made from an intricate **netting**."

Write a sentence using **netting**.

_____

_____

c. **Tatting** can mean a <u>delicate fabric woven in patterns</u>. For example, "The sleeves of Janice's shirt were made from silk **tatting**."

Write a sentence using **tatting**.

_____

_____

2 A second meaning of **lace** includes the following related words.

a. **Flavor** can mean to <u>add a small amount</u>. For example, "Lisa liked to **flavor** her soda with lemon juice."

Write a sentence using **flavor**.

_____

_____

b. **Season** can mean to <u>add a small amount</u>. For example, "I asked my mom to **season** my hot chocolate with raspberry flavoring."

Write a sentence using **season**.

_____

_____

c. **Spike** can mean to <u>add a small amount</u>. For example, "Grandpa would always **spike** his chili with hot peppers."

Write a sentence using **spike**.

_____

_____

3 A third meaning of **lace** includes the following related words.

a. **Bind** can mean to <u>tie together</u>. For example, "At the end of the semester, the art teacher had all of the students **bind** their work together into an album."

Write a sentence using **bind**.

_____

_____

b. **Fasten** can mean to <u>tie together</u>. For example, "My little brother just learned how to **fasten** his own shoes."

Write a sentence using **fasten**.

_____

_____

c. **Secure** can mean to <u>tie together</u>. For example, "Dad used a rope to **secure** the Christmas tree to the top of the car."

Write a sentence using **secure**.

_____

_____

Word Meaning in Context

Lace began in the Old French language as a word meaning "noose." Later, in the English language, this meaning expanded to include three current meanings:

- ❏ **delicate fabric woven in patterns**
- ❏ **add a small amount**
- ❏ **tie together**

1. The teacher reminded her students to **lace** up their shoes before going to play outside.

Which of the meanings of **lace** is this? _____

_____

2. My mother placed a **lace** cover over the pillows on the couch.

Which of the meanings of **lace** is this? _____

_____

3. On Thanksgiving, my grandma would **lace** the eggnog with cinnamon and nutmeg.

Which of the meanings of **lace** is this? _____

_____

Word Meaning Map   The teacher will give you the **Lace** worksheet.

Complete Each Definition

1. **Lace** can mean to fasten or _____ together.

2. **Lace** can also mean a delicate _____ or material woven into patterns.

3. **Lace** can also mean to add a _____ amount of a substance to something.

Understanding Check

Circle whether **lace** is used as you would expect.

1. After ice skating all morning on the pond with her friends, Grace wanted to go home for lunch. Before she could walk home though, she needed to **lace** up her skates and put on her shoes.

Expect   Not Expect

2. Jimmy thought the iced tea was very bland. He decided to **lace** it with a teaspoon of sugar to make it taste better.

Expect   Not Expect

3. My dad doesn't like putting anything in his coffee. When he orders coffee at a diner, he always asks them to **lace** it with sugar and cream.

Expect   Not Expect

4. Kayla was learning how to knit from her grandmother. The first thing she made was a shawl with **lace**.

Expect   Not Expect

5. My uncle still uses his old wool army blanket. The blanket has lasted for years because it was made of a durable **lace**.

Expect   Not Expect

6. My brother forgot to **lace** up his shoes when he got dressed this morning. When he came down the stairs for breakfast, he stepped on his shoestrings and tripped.

Expect   Not Expect

Create Stories

On a sheet of paper, write a short story or scenario for each of the three meanings of **lace**.

TARGET WORD

Pre-Lesson Activity—Meanings of Related Words

1 One meaning of **lap** includes the following related words.

a. **Drink** can mean to <u>take in liquid or food with the tongue</u>. For example, "After playing fetch with my dog in the park, he would always **drink** water from the lake."

Write a sentence using **drink**.

_____

_____

b. **Sip** can mean to <u>take in liquid or food with the tongue</u>. For example, "The young kitten would **sip** the milk from her bowl."

Write a sentence using **sip**.

_____

_____

c. **Eat** can mean to <u>take in liquid or food with the tongue</u>. For example, "The old stray cat would **eat** her food very slowly because she had lost several teeth."

Write a sentence using **eat**.

_____

_____

2 A second meaning of **lap** includes the following related words.

a. **Circle** can mean the <u>complete length of a race course</u>. For example, "The coach told the runners that they had to run a **circle** around the track."

Write a sentence using **circle**.

_____

_____

b. **Loop** can mean the <u>complete length of a race course</u>. For example, "At the Indianapolis 500 race track, each **loop** is two miles long."

Write a sentence using **loop**.

_____

_____

c. **Circuit** can mean the <u>complete length of a race course</u>. For example, "The horse ran the **circuit** at a record pace."

Write a sentence using **circuit**.

_____

_____

3 A third meaning of **lap** includes the following related words.

a. **Splash** can mean to <u>wash against</u>. For example, "Our hotel was so close to the beach that we could hear the **splash** of the waves from our room."

Write a sentence using **splash**.

_____

_____

b. **Beat** can mean to <u>wash against</u>. For example, "The waves continued to **beat** against the side of the sailboat as it crossed the bay."

Write a sentence using **beat**.

_____

_____

c. **Slap** can mean to <u>wash against</u>. For example, "The **slap** of waves against the dock continued to intensify as the storm approached."

Write a sentence using **slap**.

_____

_____

4 A fourth meaning of **lap** has no related words.

a. When **lap** is used in this way, it means the <u>area from the waist to the knees of a seated person</u>. For example, "All of the young children wanted to sit in Santa's **lap** and tell him what they wanted for Christmas."

Write a sentence using **lap**.

_____

_____

Word Meaning in Context

Lap began in the Old German language as a word meaning "cloth or rag." Later, in the English language, the meanings expanded to include four current meanings:

- ❑ take in liquid or food with the tongue
- ❑ complete length of a race course
- ❑ wash against
- ❑ area from the waist to knees of a seated person

1. I like to sit on my mom's **lap** when I practice reading to her.

   Which of the meanings of **lap** is this? _____

   _____

2. I could hear the cat **lap** her water when she ran in the house after being outside all day.

   Which of the meanings of **lap** is this? _____

   _____

3. The winner of the stock car race took a victory **lap** after he passed the checkered flag.

   Which of the meanings of **lap** is this? _____

   _____

4. My baby brother likes to splash water while taking a bath to see the water **lap** against the sides of the tub.

   Which of the meanings of **lap** is this? _____

   _____

Word Meaning Map   The teacher will give you the **Lap** worksheet.

Complete Each Definition

1. **Lap** can mean a complete _____ or loop of a race course.

2. **Lap** can also mean to drink or take in liquid or food with the _____

   _____.

3. **Lap** can also mean to _____ or splash against.

4. **Lap** can also mean the area from the waist to the knees of a _____ person.

Understanding Check

Circle whether **lap** is used as you would expect.

1. On Christmas Eve, my grandfather reads *The Night Before Christmas* aloud. All of the grandchildren hope they will get to sit on his **lap** and turn the pages for him as he reads.   Expect   Not Expect

2. My dog Husker was very sick last night. He refused to eat or drink anything but would **lap** at everything we tried to feed him.   Expect   Not Expect

3. Carey went to the city pool to go swimming with her friends. While she was there, they all raced a **lap** to see who the fastest swimmer was.   Expect   Not Expect

4. Rich spent the day at the lake ice fishing with his father. The lake was completely frozen. He could hear the water **lap** against the shore as he fished from a hole in the ice.   Expect   Not Expect

5. Kayley stepped on a piece of gum in the street. She didn't think she'd ever be able to get the gum off the bottom of her **lap**.   Expect   Not Expect

6. The gazelle went down to the lake at night for a drink of water. The animal would **lap** up the water while keeping a look out for danger.   Expect   Not Expect

7. The Formula One race car driver needed gas and a change of tires for the car. The driver pulled off the track and into the **lap** to have the crew work on the car.   Expect   Not Expect

8. David went fishing on a small boat with his dad. When they anchored offshore, the only noise they could hear was the **lap** of the waves against their boat.   Expect   Not Expect

Create Stories

On a sheet of paper, write a short story or scenario for each of the four meanings of **lap**.

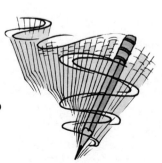

The Multiple Meaning Vocabulary Program

Pre-Lesson Activity—Meanings of Related Words

1 One meaning of **lash** includes the following related words.

a. **Batter** can mean to <u>strike</u>. For example, "The boxer attempted to **batter** his opponent."

Write a sentence using **batter**.

_____

_____

b. **Beat** can mean to <u>strike</u>. For example, "The grizzly bear used his huge paws to **beat** at other bears who were invading his territory."

Write a sentence using **beat**.

_____

_____

c. **Thrash** can mean to <u>strike</u>. For example, "The cat played with the dog by using its paw to **thrash** at him from under the couch."

Write a sentence using **thrash**.

_____

_____

2 A second meaning of **lash** includes the following related words.

a. **Bullwhip** can mean a <u>type of whip</u>. For example, "The rancher had a **bullwhip** tied to his horse's saddle."

Write a sentence using **bullwhip**.

_____

_____

b. **Switch** can mean a <u>type of whip</u>. For example, "Grandpa always threatened to use a **switch** on us if he ever heard us swear."

Write a sentence using **switch**.

_____

_____

c. **Horse whip** can mean a <u>type of whip</u>. For example, "The cowboy used a **horse whip** to corral the wild mustangs."

Write a sentence using **horse whip**.

_____

_____

3 A third meaning of **lash** includes the following related words.

a. **Fasten** can mean to <u>tie down</u>. For example, "The pilot told the passengers to **fasten** their seatbelts."

Write a sentence using **fasten**.

_____

_____

b. **Bind** can mean to <u>tie down</u>. For example, "The bank teller needed to **bind** the stacks of hundred-dollar bills at the end of the day."

Write a sentence using **bind**.

_____

_____

c. **Hitch** can mean to <u>tie down</u>. For example, "The young cowgirl learned how to **hitch** a horse to the post on her first day at the dude ranch."

Write a sentence using **hitch**.

_____

_____

4 A fourth meaning of **lash** has no related words.

a. When **lash** is used in this way, it means an <u>eyelash</u>. For example, "A **lash** from her eye was stuck on her cheek."

Write a sentence using **lash**.

_____

_____

Word Meaning in Context

Lash began in the Old English language as a word meaning "deal a blow."
Later, this meaning expanded to include four current meanings:

- ❏ strike
- ❏ type of whip
- ❏ tie down
- ❏ eyelash

1. I had a **lash** in my eye that made my eye water.

Which of the meanings of **lash** is this? _____

_____

2. My brother helped me **lash** my overstuffed suitcase by sitting on it.

Which of the meanings of **lash** is this? _____

_____

3. In the horror movie, the woman tried to **lash** out at her attacker.

Which of the meanings of **lash** is this? _____

_____

4. Cowboys use a **lash** to help them herd cattle on the ranch.

Which of the meanings of **lash** is this? _____

_____

Word Meaning Map   The teacher will give you the **Lash** worksheet.

Complete Each Definition

1. **Lash** can mean to beat or _____.

2. **Lash** can also mean a type of switch or _____.

3. **Lash** can also mean to fasten or _____ down.

4. **Lash** can also mean an _____ that helps keep dirt out of your eye.

Understanding Check

Circle whether **lash** is used as you would expect.

1. Timmy and James never really liked each other. Every time they passed each other in the school hallway, they would **lash** out at each other verbally.

    Expect   Not Expect

2. The rock concert was extremely loud and hurt everyone's ears. When Jonathan got outside of the theater, he rubbed his **lash**, which was still ringing.

    Expect   Not Expect

3. Carol couldn't wait to see her old friend again. The minute she saw her, she made sure to **lash** out at her.

    Expect   Not Expect

4. Diana kept squinting and rubbing her eyes all morning. She thought she might have a **lash** stuck in her eye.

    Expect   Not Expect

5. The ship was preparing to head into heavy seas. The skipper told the crew to **lash** down any loose items.

    Expect   Not Expect

6. Today, very few people ride a horse bareback. Most riders use either a western or English **lash** when they ride a horse.

    Expect   Not Expect

7. James needed to **lash** the bundle with rope. He laid the rope over the bundle and walked away.

    Expect   Not Expect

8. The rancher was trying to herd the cattle into the pen. He used a **lash** to help keep all of the cows together.

    Expect   Not Expect

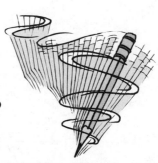

Create Stories

On a sheet of paper, write a short story or scenario for each of the four meanings of **lash**.

 ## Pre-Lesson Activity—Meanings of Related Words

1 One meaning of **limit** includes the following related words.

a. **Endpoint** can mean a <u>boundary surrounding a specific area</u>. For example, "The northern **endpoint** for the state of Washington is Canada."

Write a sentence using **endpoint**.

_____

_____

b. **Cutoff point** can mean a <u>boundary surrounding a specific area</u>. For example, "The southern **cutoff point** of Arizona is the Mexican border."

Write a sentence using **cutoff point**.

_____

_____

c. **Perimeter** can mean a <u>boundary surrounding a specific area</u>. For example, "The city zoo's **perimeter** is encircled by a 12-foot chain-link fence."

Write a sentence using **perimeter**.

_____

_____

2 A second meaning of **limit** includes the following related words.

a. **Maximum** can mean the <u>greatest amount allowed or possible</u>. For example, "Most bank ATMs have a **maximum** of two withdrawals per day for each customer."

Write a sentence using **maximum**.

_____

_____

b. **Highest** can mean the <u>greatest amount allowed or possible</u>. For example, "The **highest** a person has ever pole-vaulted is nearly 20 feet."

Write a sentence using **highest**.

_____

_____

c. **Ceiling** can mean the <u>greatest amount allowed or possible</u>. For example, "Two hundred dollars was the **ceiling** that Peter was willing to pay for the used mountain bike."

Write a sentence using **ceiling**.

_____

_____

3 A third meaning of **limit** includes the following related words.

a. **Confine** can mean to <u>restrict</u>. For example, "The teacher told the students to **confine** themselves to the playground while playing hide and seek."

Write a sentence using **confine**.

_____

_____

b. **Hinder** can mean to <u>restrict</u>. For example, "Luanne thought her mother was trying to **hinder** her fashion sense by telling her what she could wear to school."

Write a sentence using **hinder**.

_____

_____

c. **Impede** can mean to <u>restrict</u>. For example, "Diane thought that having her older brother chaperone her first date would **impede** her ability to have fun."

Write a sentence using **impede**.

_____

_____

Word Meaning in Context

Limit began in the Old French language as a word meaning "a boundary or embankment between fields." Later, in the English language, the meanings expanded to include three current meanings:

- ❏ **boundary surrounding a specific area**
- ❏ **greatest amount allowed or possible**
- ❏ **restrict**

1. My father said I had to **limit** the time I spent talking on the phone.

Which of the meanings of **limit** is this? _____

_____

2. The property **limit** of my grandfather's farm extends all the way to the interstate.

Which of the meanings of **limit** is this? _____

_____

3. There was a sign posted inside the elevator stating its weight **limit** was 1,000 pounds.

Which of the meanings of **limit** is this? _____

_____

Word Meaning Map   The teacher will give you the **Limit** worksheet.

Complete Each Definition

1. **Limit** can mean to confine or _____.

2. **Limit** can also mean a border or _____ surrounding a specific area.

3. **Limit** can also mean the maximum or _____ amount allowed or possible.

Understanding Check

Circle whether **limit** is used as you would expect.

1. The cowboys put up a barbed-wire fence around their ranch to keep the cattle from wandering off. The fence marks the **limit** of their property.

   Expect   Not Expect

2. The road sign warned that all trucks over 15 feet high could not use the tunnel. The truck driver knew his truck was at the **limit** because it was 12 feet high.

   Expect   Not Expect

3. The toy slide outside the kindergarten classroom is made for very young children. It has a weight **limit** of 50 pounds, so older children who weigh more might break it.

   Expect   Not Expect

4. Scientists claim that outer space is never ending. If you look through a telescope, you will be able to see the **limit** of outer space.

   Expect   Not Expect

5. Jill's favorite dessert is homemade apple pie. Whenever her mother bakes one, she has to **limit** Jill to two helpings, or she'll eat the entire pie.

   Expect   Not Expect

6. Roberta's father told her that she was allowed to buy any dress she wanted for her birthday party. She was so excited that her father put a **limit** on her choice of dresses.

   Expect   Not Expect

Create Stories

On a sheet of paper, write a short story or scenario for each of the three meanings of **limit**.

Litter

Pre-Lesson Activity—Meanings of Related Words

1 One meaning of **litter** includes the following related words.

a. **Trash** can mean <u>scattered garbage</u>. For example, "The empty parking lot was covered with **trash**."

Write a sentence using **trash**.

_____

_____

b. **Debris** can mean <u>scattered garbage</u>. For example, "**Debris** could be seen blowing across the highway."

Write a sentence using **debris**.

_____

_____

c. **Refuse** can mean <u>scattered garbage</u>. For example, "The alley behind the restaurant was covered with **refuse**."

Write a sentence using **refuse**.

_____

_____

2 A second meaning of **litter** includes the following related words.

a. **Clutch** can mean <u>multiple offspring produced at one birth</u>. For example, "Grandpa's prized hen hatched a **clutch** of baby chicks this morning."

Write a sentence using **clutch**.

_____

_____

b. **Young** can mean <u>multiple offspring produced at one birth</u>. For example, "The mother bear will protect her **young** until they can fend for themselves."

Write a sentence using **young**.

_____

_____

c. **Brood** can mean <u>multiple offspring produced at one birth</u>. For example, "The **brood** of kittens clung to their mother looking for food."
Write a sentence using **brood**.

_____

_____

3 A third meaning of **litter** includes the following related words.

a. **Floor covering** can mean a <u>bedding for animals</u>. For example, "Willy changes the **floor covering** in his gerbil's cage every week."
Write a sentence using **floor covering**.

_____

_____

b. **Straw** can mean a <u>bedding for animals</u>. For example, "The floor of the horse stall was covered with **straw**."
Write a sentence using **straw**.

_____

_____

c. **Shavings** can mean a <u>bedding for animals</u>. For example, "The lizards were sleeping on the **shavings** in their terrarium."
Write a sentence using **shavings**.

_____

_____

4 A fourth meaning of **litter** includes the following related words.

a. **Stretcher** can mean <u>something for carrying an injured person</u>. For example, "The paramedics carried the man to the ambulance on a **stretcher**."
Write a sentence using **stretcher**.

_____

_____

b. **Carrier** can mean <u>something for carrying an injured person</u>. For example, "The ski patrol used a **carrier** to bring the injured skier down the mountain."
Write a sentence using **carrier**.

_____

_____

c. **Travois** can mean <u>something for carrying an injured person</u>. For example, "Native Americans used a **travois** to carry supplies and injured people when they moved for the season."
Write a sentence using **travois**.

_____

_____

Word Meaning in Context

Litter began in the Latin language as a word meaning "bed." Later, in the English language, this meaning expanded to include four current meanings:

- ❑ scattered garbage
- ❑ multiple offspring produced at one birth
- ❑ bedding for animals
- ❑ something for carrying an injured person

1. When the trash can turned over, **litter** spilled all over the street.

Which of the meanings of **litter** is this? _____

_____

2. The lifeguards kept a **litter** near the guard tower in case of an emergency.

Which of the meanings of **litter** is this? _____

_____

3. Jason's Siamese cat had a **litter** of nine kittens last night.

Which of the meanings of **litter** is this? _____

_____

4. The kennel manager changes the **litter** in the puppies' kennel several times per day.

Which of the meanings of **litter** is this? _____

_____

Word Meaning Map   The teacher will give you the **Litter** worksheet.

Complete Each Definition

1. **Litter** can mean scattered _____ or trash.

2. **Litter** can also mean multiple _____, such as puppies, produced at one birth.

3. **Litter** can also mean a _____ or floor covering for animals.

4. **Litter** can also mean something used for _____ an injured person such as a stretcher.

Understanding Check

Circle whether **litter** is used as you would expect.

1. The football stadium is filthy after every game. Workers are hired to pick up **litter** and debris once the fans leave.

   Expect   Not Expect

2. It was Michelle's turn to take care of her family's guinea pig. She fed him a half cup of **litter** and filled his bowl with water.

   Expect   Not Expect

3. The Doberman Pinscher gave birth to a half dozen puppies last month. The **litter** will be sold once they are 16 weeks old.

   Expect   Not Expect

4. Deborah spent all morning cleaning her bedroom. When she finished, her parents complimented her on how nice the **litter** looked in her room.

   Expect   Not Expect

5. My oldest sister just gave birth to a baby boy. She promised to send me pictures of the **litter** once she returns from the hospital.

   Expect   Not Expect

6. Kyle broke his leg while playing soccer. The coaches carried him off the field on a **litter**.

   Expect   Not Expect

7. Louise just received a hamster for her birthday. She was busy putting fresh **litter** in the hamster's cage.

   Expect   Not Expect

8. Denise twisted her ankle while skateboarding. The doctor applied ice to the injury and then wrapped it in a **litter** to help with the swelling.

   Expect   Not Expect

Create Stories

On a sheet of paper, write a short story or scenario for each of the four meanings of **litter**.

Lodge

Pre-Lesson Activity—Meanings of Related Words

1 One meaning of **lodge** includes the following related words.

a. **Cabin** can mean a <u>type of shelter</u>. For example, "Uncle Bob has a small **cabin** in Alaska that he uses for hunting."
Write a sentence using **cabin**.

_____

_____

b. **Cottage** can mean a <u>type of shelter</u>. For example, "Every winter, my family vacations for a week in a **cottage** on the beach in Florida."
Write a sentence using **cottage**.

_____

_____

c. **Chalet** can mean a <u>type of shelter</u>. For example, "My father wants to rent a ski **chalet** in Colorado during Christmas break."
Write a sentence using **chalet**.

_____

_____

2 A second meaning of **lodge** includes the following related words.

a. **Fraternity** can mean an <u>association of people with similar interests</u>. For example, "My older brother joined a **fraternity** when he went away to college."
Write a sentence using **fraternity**.

_____

_____

b. **Club** can mean an <u>association of people with similar interests</u>. For example, "Mom makes fun of dad every time he wears his moose hat from the men's **club** he joined."
Write a sentence using **club**.

_____

_____

c. **Sorority** can mean an <u>association of people with similar interests</u>. For example, "The homecoming queen was also the president of her **sorority**."
Write a sentence using **sorority**.

_____

_____

3 A third meaning of **lodge** includes the following related words.

a. **Register** can mean to <u>submit</u>. For example, "After the man received a speeding ticket from the police officer, he said he would **register** a complaint."
Write a sentence using **register**.

_____

_____

b. **File** can mean to <u>submit</u>. For example, "After the car accident, my dad called the insurance company to **file** a claim."
Write a sentence using **file**.

_____

_____

c. **Record** can mean to <u>submit</u>. For example, "Sam worked at the customer service department helping customers who want to **record** a complaint."
Write a sentence using **record**.

_____

_____

4 A fourth meaning of **lodge** includes the following related words.

a. **Become embedded** can mean to <u>implant</u>. For example, "The bow hunter missed the deer, and his arrow had **become embedded** in a tree."
Write a sentence using **become embedded**.

_____

_____

b. **Stick** can mean to <u>implant</u>. For example, "High winds from the hurricane caused a broken tree branch to **stick** into the side of the house."
Write a sentence using **stick**.

_____

_____

c. **Become caught** can mean to <u>implant</u>. For example, "The kite had **become caught** in the tree branches."
Write a sentence using **become caught**.

_____

_____

Word Meaning in Context

Lodge began in the German language as a word meaning "summer house." Later, in the English language, this meaning expanded to include four current meanings:

- ❑ **type of shelter**
- ❑ **association of people with similar interests**
- ❑ **submit**
- ❑ **implant**

1. Artie and his family spent the summer at a **lodge** in the mountains.

Which of the meanings of **lodge** is this? _____

_____

2. The dart's tip was very dull so it wouldn't **lodge** in the dartboard properly.

Which of the meanings of **lodge** is this? _____

_____

3. Tom's father is a member of the Moose's **lodge**.

Which of the meanings of **lodge** is this? _____

_____

4. The customer was very upset with the service she received at the store and wanted to **lodge** a complaint.

Which of the meanings of **lodge** is this? _____

_____

Word Meaning Map   The teacher will give you the **Lodge** worksheet.

Complete Each Definition

1. Lodge can mean a type of _____ or house.

2. Lodge can also mean an _____ or club for people with similar interests.

3. Lodge can also mean to register or _____ something such as a complaint.

4. Lodge can also mean to _____ or embed something.

✓ Understanding Check

Circle whether **lodge** is used as you would expect.

1. Dad spends every Thursday night with his friends. He and his friends are all members of the Elk's **lodge**.

   Expect   Not Expect

2. My brother and I like to sleep out under the stars in our backyard. We roll out our sleeping bags on the grassy **lodge** and enjoyed the evening sky.

   Expect   Not Expect

3. Christy went with her family to the mountains for the weekend. She said they stayed in a rustic **lodge** with no electricity.

   Expect   Not Expect

4. Tonya dribbled the basketball down the court. The ball would **lodge** into the wooden court on every bounce.

   Expect   Not Expect

5. The electricity kept shutting off at our house last night. My mother called the power company to **lodge** a complaint.

   Expect   Not Expect

6. John received a letter with an entry form in the mail stating that he might be the winner of a million dollars. After he tore up the letter and entry forms, he made sure to **lodge** all of the forms.

   Expect   Not Expect

7. I don't like to ride my bike by the lumberyard. I'm always afraid a splinter will **lodge** into my tire and cause a flat.

   Expect   Not Expect

8. While on vacation, Wilma met a stranger who grew up in the same state she did. She was amazed they both grew up in the same **lodge**.

   Expect   Not Expect

Create Stories

On a sheet of paper, write a short story or scenario for each of the four meanings of **lodge**.

TARGET WORD |  **Lump**

 ## Pre-Lesson Activity—Meanings of Related Words

1 One meaning of **lump** includes the following related words.

a. **Hunk** can mean an <u>irregularly shaped mass</u>. For example, "The butcher placed a **hunk** of meat into a package for his customer."

Write a sentence using **hunk**.

_____

_____

b. **Piece** can mean an <u>irregularly shaped mass</u>. For example, "The miner picked up a **piece** of shiny rock from the floor of the mine shaft."

Write a sentence using **piece**.

_____

_____

c. **Clump** can mean an <u>irregularly shaped mass</u>. For example, "Kimberly was afraid she might be getting a **clump** of coal in her Christmas stocking for lying to her little brother."

Write a sentence using **clump**.

_____

_____

2 A second meaning of **lump** includes the following related words.

a. **Group** can mean to <u>put together</u>. For example, "Daniel liked to **group** all of his crayons into one shoe box."

Write a sentence using **group**.

_____

_____

c. **Combine** can mean to <u>put together</u>. For example, "The cookbook said to cut up all the vegetables then **combine** them with the chicken before cooking."

Write a sentence using **combine**.

_____

_____

d. **Pool** can mean to <u>put together</u>. For example, "The class tried to **pool** their ideas to come up with a fun theme for the school dance."

Write a sentence using **pool**.

_____

_____

3 A third meaning of **lump** includes the following related words.

a. **Bruise** can mean a <u>swelling on the body</u>. For example, "After banging her arm into the doorknob, Diane saw a **bruise** on her elbow."

Write a sentence using **bruise**.

_____

_____

b. **Injury** can mean a <u>swelling on the body</u>. For example, "Grace received an **injury** on her knee from falling while playing basketball with her brothers."

Write a sentence using **injury**.

_____

_____

c. **Contusion** can mean a <u>swelling on the body</u>. For example, "My dad got a **contusion** from hitting his head on the doorway."

Write a sentence using **contusion**.

_____

_____

4 A fourth meaning of **lump** has no related words.

a. When **lump** is used in this way, it means a <u>small cube of sugar</u>. For example, "The waiter asked grandma if she wanted one **lump** or two in her tea."

Write a sentence using **lump**.

_____

_____

Word Meaning in Context

Lump began in the German language as a word meaning "shapeless things." Later, in the English language, the meaning expanded to include four current meanings:

- ❏ irregularly shaped mass
- ❏ put together
- ❏ swelling on the body
- ❏ small cube of sugar

1. Aunt Mary always put one **lump** into her glass of iced tea to make it sweeter.

   Which of the meanings of **lump** is this? _____

   _____

2. Tina had a doctor look at the **lump** in her arm.

   Which of the meanings of **lump** is this? _____

   _____

3. Beverly asked her mother if she could **lump** all of the different types of cookies together into one jar.

   Which of the meanings of **lump** is this? _____

   _____

4. The coyote in the cartoon had a huge **lump** on his head after he ran into the side of a mountain.

   Which of the meanings of **lump** is this? _____

   _____

Word Meaning Map   The teacher will give you the **Lump** worksheet.

Complete Each Definition

1. **Lump** can mean an irregularly shaped _____
   or piece of matter.

2. **Lump** can also mean to put or group _____.

3. **Lump** can also mean a _____ on the body.

4. **Lump** can also mean a small cube of _____ or sweetener.

Understanding Check

Circle whether **lump** is used as you would expect.

1. Sean let out a yelp after he bumped his head on the desk after reaching down to pick up his pencil. When he stood up, he had a good-sized **lump** on his head.

   Expect   Not Expect

2. Jill tried making mashed potatoes for the first time. She did not whip the potatoes for very long, and everyone who ate them said there was a **lump** or two in them.

   Expect   Not Expect

3. Charlie bumped his head on the kitchen doorway several years ago. It has since completely healed and left him with a smooth **lump**.

   Expect   Not Expect

4. Jonathan enjoys playing marbles with his friends. They shoot the **lumps** of glass for hours and trade each other for their favorite colors.

   Expect   Not Expect

5. Mrs. Jones is a great music teacher who believes every student learns at a different pace. She always tries to **lump** her students together when she is teaching because she believes they are so unique.

   Expect   Not Expect

6. Susan was making sugar cookies for her friend's birthday party. She added one **lump** of sugar to the dough to make a hundred cookies.

   Expect   Not Expect

7. Chris is trying to collect all of the 50 state quarters that are being minted. Until he can get a display case for them, he thought he would just **lump** them together in his piggy bank upstairs.

   Expect   Not Expect

8. Grandpa likes Beth's lemonade but thinks it is too tart. He always adds a **lump** of sugar to his glass for a sweeter flavor.

   Expect   Not Expect

Create Stories

On a sheet of paper, write a short story or scenario for each of the four meanings of **lump**.

 Pre-Lesson Activity—Meanings of Related Words

1 One meaning of **lying** includes the following related words.

   a. **Deceitful** can mean <u>misleading</u>. For example, "Greg's **deceitful** ways made it very difficult for his family and friends to believe anything he said."
   Write a sentence using **deceitful**.

   _____

   _____

   b. **Dishonest** can mean <u>misleading</u>. For example, "Lyle's **dishonest** remarks about his classmates made everyone wonder what he was saying about them behind their backs."
   Write a sentence using **dishonest**.

   _____

   _____

   c. **Untrustworthy** can mean <u>misleading</u>. For example, "The principal said Jim's **untrustworthy** ways would make others not believe him when he really needed them."
   Write a sentence using **untrustworthy**.

   _____

   _____

2 A second meaning of **lying** includes the following related words.

   a. **White lie** can mean a <u>known false statement</u>. For example, "The **white lie** Jake told to his friends was not meant to hurt anyone."
   Write a sentence using **white lie**.

   _____

   _____

   b. **Tall tale** can mean a <u>known false statement</u>. For example, "Miguel's friends thought his **tall tale** about meeting up with a bear while camping was very entertaining."
   Write a sentence using **tall tale**.

   _____

   _____

c. **Perjury** can mean a <u>known false statement</u>. For example, "The judge warned the witness she could be charged with **perjury** if she kept changing her story about the accident." Write a sentence using **perjury**.

_____

_____

3 A third meaning of **lying** includes the following related words.

a. **Fibbing** can mean <u>speaking falsely to deceive</u>. For example, "Lance's mom knew he was **fibbing** about not eating the cookies because there was chocolate all over his face." Write a sentence using **fibbing**.

_____

_____

b. **Misleading** can mean <u>speaking falsely to deceive</u>. For example, "Candice was intentionally **misleading** her mother when she said that she didn't have any homework." Write a sentence using **misleading**.

_____

_____

c. **Hoodwinking** can mean <u>speaking falsely to deceive</u>. For example, "The class tried **hoodwinking** the substitute teacher by telling him they got an hour of recess every day." Write a sentence using **hoodwinking**.

_____

_____

4 A fourth meaning of **lying** includes the following related words.

a. **Reclining** can mean <u>resting in a flat or horizontal position</u>. For example, "My grandpa was reclining on the sofa after he mowed the lawn." Write a sentence using **reclining**.

_____

_____

b. **Lounging** can mean <u>resting in a flat or horizontal position</u>. For example, "Grace was **lounging** around the den, waiting for her friends to call her back."
Write a sentence using **lounging**.

_____

_____

c. **Sprawled** can mean <u>resting in a flat or horizontal position</u>. For example, "The kindergarten class was **sprawled** across the floor watching a video."

Write a sentence using **sprawled**.

_____

_____

Word Meaning in Context

Lying began in the Old English language as a word meaning "speak falsely." Later, the meaning expanded to include four current meanings:

- ❏ **misleading**
- ❏ **known false statement**
- ❏ **speaking falsely to deceive**
- ❏ **resting in a flat or horizontal position**

1. Ed's **lying** ways kept him from making many close friends at school.

Which of the meanings of **lying** is this? _____

_____

2. The little boy's constant **lying** seemed to always get him into trouble.

Which of the meanings of **lying** is this? _____

_____

3. The policeman knew John was **lying** when he said he wasn't speeding.

Which of the meanings of **lying** is this? _____

_____

4. Laura was **lying** down in the recliner watching TV.

Which of the meanings of **lying** is this? _____

_____

Word Meaning Map   The teacher will give you the **Lying** worksheet.

Complete Each Definition

1. **Lying** can mean being dishonest or _____.

2. **Lying** can also mean making a known _____ statement.

3. **Lying** can also mean talking or _____ falsely to deceive.

4. **Lying** can also mean _____ or reclining in a flat or horizontal position.

Understanding Check

Circle whether **lying** is used as you would expect.

1. William just got back from a long jog. He was in the living room **lying** on the floor trying to cool down.

   Expect   Not Expect

2. Mike was scared he was going to get a ticket for driving through a red light. He thought about **lying** when the police officer asked him if he saw the light change colors before he drove through the intersection.

   Expect   Not Expect

3. The prosecuting attorney asked the defendant the same question several times while he was on the witness stand. She was hoping he would change his answer so she could accuse him of **lying**.

   Expect   Not Expect

4. When witnesses take the stand in a court of law, they swear an oath that they will tell the truth. It is very important for every witness to promise they will be **lying** when questioned by the court.

   Expect   Not Expect

5. The marching band was performing on the football field during the halftime show. During the performance, the band members were **lying** on the field playing their instruments.

   Expect   Not Expect

6. The senator is a very honest man. He is best known for his **lying** while serving in our nation's capital.

   Expect   Not Expect

7. Zachary is well known for exaggerating the truth whenever he tells a story. He says his **lying** helps him tell entertaining stories.

   Expect   Not Expect

8. The preacher was well known and respected for always speaking the truth. His friends and neighbors admired him for his **lying** ways.

   Expect   Not Expect

Create Stories

On a sheet of paper, write a short story or scenario for each of the four meanings of **lying**.

 **Major**

 # Pre-Lesson Activity—Meanings of Related Words

1 One meaning of **major** includes the following related words.

    a. **Larger** can mean <u>greater in number, size, or extent</u>. For example, "A **larger** portion of the city's population now lives in the suburbs."

       Write a sentence using **larger**.

       _____

       _____

    b. **Dominant** can mean <u>greater in number, size, or extent</u>. For example, "The team captain was the **dominant** player on the basketball team."

       Write a sentence using **dominant**.

       _____

       _____

    c. **Chief** can mean <u>greater in number, size, or extent</u>. For example, "The **chief** complaint from most students was that they were not allowed to eat lunch off campus."

       Write a sentence using **chief**.

       _____

       _____

2 A second meaning of **major** includes the following related words.

    a. **Degree** can mean a <u>field of study</u>. For example, "Mr. Smith's **degree** was in math, so he really enjoys teaching that class period."

       Write a sentence using **degree**.

       _____

       _____

b. **Academic interest** can mean a <u>field of study</u>. For example, "The school counselor asked all of the students to think about what **academic interest** they might want to pursue in college."

Write a sentence using **academic interest**.

_____

_____

c. **Coursework** can mean a <u>field of study</u>. For example, "My sister wants to be a doctor, so her college **coursework** is in science."

Write a sentence using **coursework**.

_____

_____

3 A third meaning of **major** has no related words.

a. When **major** is used in this way, it means an <u>officer's rank in the military</u>. For example, "The Air Force **major** climbed into the cockpit of her F-16 fighter to fly a combat mission."

Write a sentence using **major**.

_____

_____

4 A fourth meaning of **major** has no related words.

a. When **major** is used in this way, it means a <u>scale in music</u>. For example, "The band argued about whether they should play the next song in D or F **major** to get the right sound they wanted."

Write a sentence using **major**.

_____

_____

Word Meaning in Context

Major began in the Latin language as a word meaning "large or great." Later, in the English language, the meanings expanded to include four current meanings:

- ❏ **greater in number, size, or extent**
- ❏ **field of study**
- ❏ **officer's rank in the military**
- ❏ **scale in music**

1. The shoe company is a **major** sponsor of many professional sporting events.

Which of the meanings of **major** is this? _____

_____

2. My brother just started college and wants to **major** in biology.

Which of the meanings of **major** is this? _____

_____

3. The Marine **major** was in charge of a battalion of tanks during the war.

Which of the meanings of **major** is this? _____

_____

4. The conductor asked the orchestra to play the next musical piece in D **major**.

Which of the meanings of **major** is this? _____

_____

Word Meaning Map   The teacher will give you the **Major** worksheet.

Complete Each Definition

1. **Major** can mean to be larger or _____ in number, size, or extent.

2. **Major** can also mean a scale in _____ for playing an instrument.

3. **Major** can also mean a person's area of interest, or field of _____.

4. **Major** can also mean an officer's _____ in the military.

Understanding Check

Circle whether **major** is used as you would expect.

1. Our entire family helped paint my grandparent's house. While the kids scraped the walls and mixed the paints, my parents did the **major** share of the painting.   Expect   Not Expect

2. Linda's father is on the Army's parachute team, the Golden Knights. He is a **major** in the Army's special forces unit.   Expect   Not Expect

3. Kurt was asked to play a small nonspeaking role in the school Christmas play. He felt comfortable that he could handle such a **major** role.   Expect   Not Expect

4. The music teacher showed the class how a song can sound different depending upon the chord it is played in. He played a song in D minor and then a second time in D **major** so we could hear the difference.   Expect   Not Expect

5. Susan loves to scuba dive and wants to study oceans when she goes to college. She would like to **major** in marine biology at the University of Hawaii.   Expect   Not Expect

6. Mrs. Kline was selected to be principal of our school next year. She was very excited about her new position as **major**.   Expect   Not Expect

7. Mike was learning how to play a musical instrument. He chose to play the **major** because he really liked the way it sounded.   Expect   Not Expect

8. Darrel enjoys drawing and hopes to become an architect when he grows up. He went to the library and found a **major** on architecture and brought it home to read.   Expect   Not Expect

Create Stories

On a sheet of paper, write a short story or scenario for each of the four meanings of **major**.

Match

Pre-Lesson Activity—Meanings of Related Words

1 One meaning of **match** includes the following related words.

    a. **Duplicate** can mean <u>one thing that is exactly like another</u>. For example, "My sister asked me if I had seen the **duplicate** of the shoe she was holding."

    Write a sentence using **duplicate**.

    _____

    _____

    b. **Mate** can mean <u>one thing that is exactly like another</u>. For example, "Glenn looked through his closet and found three gloves, all without a **mate**."

    Write a sentence using **mate**.

    _____

    _____

    c. **Spitting image** can mean <u>one thing that is exactly like another</u>. For example, "Each of the two bookends was the **spitting image** of the other."

    Write a sentence using **spitting image**.

    _____

    _____

2 A second meaning of **match** includes the following related words.

    a. **Union** can mean a <u>marriage or relationship</u>. For example, "The young couple held a party to celebrate their recent **union**."

    Write a sentence using **union**.

    _____

    _____

b. **Pairing** can mean a <u>marriage or relationship</u>. For example, "All of Jessica's friends thought her recent **pairing** with Bob was a bad idea because they had very different personalities."

Write a sentence using **pairing**.

_____

_____

c. **Partnership** can mean a <u>marriage or relationship</u>. For example, "The couple's **partnership** lasted for over 20 years."

Write a sentence using **partnership**.

_____

_____

3 A third meaning of **match** includes the following related words.

a. **Tournament** can mean a <u>competition</u>. For example, "The boxing **tournament** was going to be televised live this evening."

Write a sentence using **tournament**.

_____

_____

b. **Contest** can mean a <u>competition</u>. For example, "The winner of the high school volleyball **contest** will be the state champion."

Write a sentence using **contest**.

_____

_____

c. **Event** can mean a <u>competition</u>. For example, "The chess **event** was held downtown at the Civic Center."

Write a sentence using **event**.

_____

_____

4 A fourth meaning of **match** has no related words.

a. When **match** is used in this way, it means an <u>easily ignited stick of wood</u>. For example, "The man at the bus stop used a **match** to light his cigar."

Write a sentence using **match**.

_____

_____

Word Meaning in Context

Match began in the Old French language as a word meaning "wick of a candle." Later, in the English language, this meaning expanded to include four current meanings:

- ❏ **one thing that is exactly like another**
- ❏ **marriage or relationship**
- ❏ **competition**
- ❏ **easily ignited stick of wood**

1. The goal for many Boy Scouts is to start a campfire without using a **match**.

Which of the meanings of **match** is this? _____

_____

2. I couldn't find the **match** to my favorite pair of socks this morning.

Which of the meanings of **match** is this? _____

_____

3. Everyone said my grandparent's relationship was a **match** made in heaven.

Which of the meanings of **match** is this? _____

_____

4. Kim saw that her next tennis **match** was against her friend Jill.

Which of the meanings of **match** is this? _____

_____

Word Meaning Map   The teacher will give you the **Match** worksheet.

Complete Each Definition

1. **Match** can mean a person or thing that is a duplicate or is _____

_____ like another person or thing.

2. **Match** can also mean a _____ or relationship.

3. **Match** can also mean a contest or _____.

4. **Match** can also mean an easily lit or ignited _____ of wood.

Understanding Check

Circle whether **match** is used as you would expect.

1. My brother accidentally broke my mother's favorite lamp. He spent the rest of the day shopping for a **match** to replace it.

   Expect   Not Expect

2. Lilly was in her older sister's wedding party. She thought her sister had found a good **match**.

   Expect   Not Expect

3. Most of Kyle's clothes were dirty, and all he could find was a clean red sock and a clean purple sock. He was frustrated because he had found a **match**.

   Expect   Not Expect

4. Kelly did not like Bill at all. Her friends knew this, so they tried to **match** them up for a date.

   Expect   Not Expect

5. James wanted to see how far professional golfers could hit the ball. He bought a ticket for the upcoming golf **match** that was being played in town next weekend.

   Expect   Not Expect

6. The waiter informed the man that smoking was not allowed inside the restaurant. The man then put his cigarette out in the **match**.

   Expect   Not Expect

7. Stephen was shooting basketballs in the backyard by himself. When he finished with his **match**, he drank some water from the kitchen.

   Expect   Not Expect

8. Ada wanted to light the candles in the living room. She used one **match** to light each of the candles.

   Expect   Not Expect

Create Stories

On a sheet of paper, write a short story or scenario for each of the four meanings of **match**.

Memory

Pre-Lesson Activity—Meanings of Related Words

1 One meaning of **memory** includes the following related words.

a. **Retention** can mean the <u>ability to recall information</u>. For example, "My grandfather has been complaining about his poor **retention** over the past several years."

Write a sentence using **retention**.

_____

_____

b. **Recognition** can mean the <u>ability to recall information</u>. For example, "The little boy's **recognition** was not very good, and he would frequently forget who his kindergarten teacher was."

Write a sentence using **recognition**.

_____

_____

c. **Cognizance** can mean the <u>ability to recall information</u>. For example, "The doctor checked the boxer's **cognizance** after he was knocked out by asking him if he knew where he was."

Write a sentence using **cognizance**.

_____

_____

2 A second meaning of **memory** includes the following related words.

a. **Flashback** can mean a <u>past event remembered</u>. For example, "The woman had a **flashback** to her car accident last year."

Write a sentence using **flashback**.

_____

_____

b. **Recollection** can mean a <u>past event remembered</u>. For example, "My mother had a **recollection** in the car about the time she got her driver's license."

Write a sentence using **recollection**

_____

_____

c. **Recall** can mean a <u>past event remembered</u>. For example, "The race car driver said he had no **recall** of what happened when his car spun out of control and crashed into the wall."

Write a sentence using **recall**.

_____

_____

3 A third meaning of **memory** includes the following related words.

a. **Storage bank** can mean the <u>part of a computer where data are stored</u>. For example, "The students kept asking the teacher if they were ever going to get a new computer with a larger **storage bank**."

Write a sentence using **storage bank**.

_____

_____

b. **Information store** can mean the <u>part of a computer where data are stored</u>. For example, "Our home computer could not run the latest video games because it does not have enough **information store** available."

Write a sentence using **information store**.

_____

_____

c. **Hard drive** can mean the <u>part of a computer where data are stored</u>. For example, "The mainframe computer used by the city school system has an extremely large capacity in its **hard drive**, especially in comparison to the average personal computer."

Write a sentence using **hard drive**.

_____

_____

4 A fourth meaning of **memory** has no related words.

a. When **memory** is used in this way, it means the <u>capacity of a material to return to a previous shape</u>. For example, "The stretch dolls are made out of rubber with **memory** so they don't bend out of shape."

Write a sentence using **memory**.

_____

_____

Word Meaning in Context

Memory began in the Old French language as a word meaning "mindful remembering." Later, in the English language, the meaning expanded to include four current meanings:

- ❑ **ability to recall information**
- ❑ **past event remembered**
- ❑ **part of a computer where data are stored**
- ❑ **capacity of a material to return to a previous shape**

1. The foam rubber football has an excellent **memory**, so it keeps its shape even after it's squished.

Which of the meanings of **memory** is this? _____

_____

2. My history teacher's **memory** is simply amazing when it comes to names and dates.

Which of the meanings of **memory** is this? _____

_____

3. Grandpa says his favorite **memory** is of when he first met grandma.

Which of the meanings of **memory** is this? _____

_____

4. My new laptop's **memory** is two gigahertz, which is large enough to run any video game.

Which of the meanings of **memory** is this? _____

_____

Word Meaning Map The teacher will give you the **Memory** worksheet.

Complete Each Definition

1. **Memory** can mean a person's retention or their ability to _____
_____ information.

2. **Memory** can also mean a flashback or past event that is _____.

3. **Memory** can also mean the storage bank or part of a computer where _____
are stored.

4. **Memory** can also mean the capacity of a material to keep or _____
to a previous shape.

Understanding Check

Circle whether **memory** is used as you would expect.

1. My parents love to watch the Jeopardy TV show. The winners always seem to have an amazing **memory** for facts.   Expect   Not Expect

2. Jill is studying for her math test tomorrow. Because of her good **memory** she frequently forgets the answers to questions.   Expect   Not Expect

3. The batter swung hard and hit the rubber softball into the outfield. The center fielder caught it and noticed that the ball had good **memory** and so it was still perfectly round.   Expect   Not Expect

4. My little brother knocked over my mother's favorite vase while playing in the house. The vase shattered into pieces because the glass had a good **memory**.   Expect   Not Expect

5. My little sister is always complaining that our family's computer is getting old. He says we should buy a new one for Christmas that has more **memory**.   Expect   Not Expect

6. Alan needed to make a presentation in front of the entire school. He had to read a poem straight from the book because he had the poem stored in his **memory**.   Expect   Not Expect

7. My parents went to their high school reunion last night. They recalled a fond **memory** of when they met at a dance in the gym.   Expect   Not Expect

8. Bruce just bought a new computer. He also bought a flat-screen **memory** so he would have excellent graphics for his video games.   Expect   Not Expect

Create Stories

On a sheet of paper, write a short story or scenario for each of the four meanings of **memory**.

Mind

Pre-Lesson Activity—Meanings of Related Words

1 One meaning of **mind** includes the following related words.

  a. **Brain** can mean the <u>part of the body that thinks</u>. For example, "Chess is a fun game to play because you have to use your **brain** before you make a move."
  Write a sentence using **brain**.

  _____

  _____

  b. **Intellect** can mean the <u>part of the body that thinks</u>. For example, "The national antidrug campaign stresses that drugs have a harmful effect on a person's **intellect**."
  Write a sentence using **intellect**.

  _____

  _____

  c. **Head** can mean the <u>part of the body that thinks</u>. For example, "The coach really liked the new linebacker because he uses his **head** to figure out what type of play the offense will run."
  Write a sentence using **head**.

  _____

  _____

2 A second meaning of **mind** includes the following related words.

  a. **Object** can mean to <u>take offense</u>. For example, "I hope my mother doesn't **object** to me eating the last piece of apple pie."
  Write a sentence using **object**.

  _____

  _____

  b. **Care** can mean to <u>take offense</u>. For example, "Cindy hoped her best friend wouldn't **care** that Cindy had just started dating her old boyfriend."
  Write a sentence using **care**.

  _____

  _____

c. **Disapprove** can mean to <u>take offense</u>. For example, "Karen thought her dad was likely to **disapprove** of her decision to go out with friends on a school night." Write a sentence using **disapprove**.

_____

_____

3 A third meaning of **mind** includes the following related words.

a. **Look after** can mean to <u>take care of</u>. For example, "My neighbor asked if I could **look after** her cat while she was gone for the weekend." Write a sentence using **look after**.

_____

_____

b. **Keep an eye on** can mean to <u>take care of</u>. For example, "Dad told me to **keep an eye on** my little brother while he went to the hardware store." Write a sentence using **keep an eye on**.

_____

_____

c. **Watch over** can mean to <u>take care of</u>. For example, "The substitute teacher was asked to **watch over** our class while our teacher went to a meeting." Write a sentence using **watch over**.

_____

_____

4 A fourth meaning of **mind** includes the following related words.

a. **Obey** can mean to <u>comply with</u>. For example, "My dog Rex never seems to **obey** my mother's commands." Write a sentence using **obey**.

_____

_____

b. **Respect** can mean to <u>comply with</u>. For example, "Mom said all of the kids needed to **respect** the baby-sitter's wishes while she and dad went out to dinner." Write a sentence using **respect**.

_____

_____

c. **Heed** can mean to <u>comply with</u>. For example, "The bus driver asked for everyone to **heed** his request and get off the bus so he could change the flat tire." Write a sentence using **heed**.

_____

_____

Word Meaning in Context

Mind began in the Old English language as a word meaning "push tightly together." Later, this meaning expanded to include four current meanings:

- ❏ **part of the body that thinks**
- ❏ **take offense**
- ❏ **take care of**
- ❏ **comply with**

1. If you read a lot of books, it will expand your **mind**.

Which of the meanings of **mind** is this? _____

_____

2. Mom asked if I would **mind** helping with the dishes after dinner.

Which of the meanings of **mind** is this? _____

_____

3. Jeff's parents asked him to **mind** the house while they went to visit a sick friend.

Which of the meanings of **mind** is this? _____

_____

4. The principal reminded us that we needed to **mind** the substitute teacher.

Which of the meanings of **mind** is this? _____

_____

Word Meaning Map   The teacher will give you the **Mind** worksheet.

Complete Each Definition

1. Mind can mean the part of the body that _____
or contains a person's intellect.

2. Mind can also mean to object or take _____.

3. Mind can also mean to look after or take _____ of something.

4. Mind can also mean to obey or _____ with.

Understanding Check

Circle whether **mind** is used as you would expect.

1. Justin was always very good at school. His parents and friends thought he had a very sharp **mind**.

   Expect   Not Expect

2. Sandy is very polite to the new students in our class. The teacher remarked about how the new students really **mind** Sandy being friendly and offering to show them around the school.

   Expect   Not Expect

3. John was at the back of the cafeteria line when the bell rang for his next class. He asked if anyone would **mind** if he cut the line so he wouldn't be late for class.

   Expect   Not Expect

4. Cindy tried hard to train her cat to sit and roll over. No matter how much she worked with the cat, it did not seem to **mind** her commands.

   Expect   Not Expect

5. Kevin fell off his bike while riding to school. The school nurse told him to put an ice pack on his knee but warned that his **mind** would probably be sore for a few days.

   Expect   Not Expect

6. My parents hate when salesmen call them at home. They always **mind** the salesmen and instead of listening to their every word, they hang up right away.

   Expect   Not Expect

7. On weekends I help my grandparents at the delicatessen they own. Sometimes they ask me to **mind** the place if they have to run errands.

   Expect   Not Expect

8. Our new neighbor down the block hasn't mowed his lawn since he moved in, and the grass is now over two feet high. The neighbors are starting to become upset that he does **mind** his lawn.

   Expect   Not Expect

Create Stories

On a sheet of paper, write a short story or scenario for each of the four meanings of **mind**.

The Multiple Meaning Vocabulary Program

Muffler

Pre-Lesson Activity—Meanings of Related Words

1 One meaning of **muffler** includes the following related words.

a. **Scarf** can mean an <u>article of clothing worn around the neck to keep warm</u>. For example, "The snowboarder wore a **scarf** to help keep the snow from getting down her coat whenever she wiped out."

Write a sentence using **scarf**.

_____

_____

b. **Neckerchief** can mean an <u>article of clothing worn around the neck to keep warm</u>. For example, "The young girl gave her mother a **neckerchief** with snowmen on it for Christmas."

Write a sentence using **neckerchief**.

_____

_____

c. **Bandanna** can mean an <u>article of clothing worn around the neck to keep warm</u>. For example, "Some motorcycle riders wear a **bandanna** under their leather jackets to help keep out the cold wind."

Write a sentence using **bandanna**.

_____

_____

2 A second meaning of **muffler** includes the following related words.

a. **Gag** can mean a <u>device used to absorb sound</u>. For example, "The bank robbers placed a **gag** on each bank teller so they couldn't yell for help."

Write a sentence using **gag**.

_____

_____

b. **Muzzle** can mean a <u>device used to absorb sound</u>. For example, "My father threatened to put a **muzzle** on the dog when he kept barking at the neighbor's cat last night."

Write a sentence using **muzzle**.

_____

_____

c. **Silencer** can mean a <u>device used to absorb sound</u>. For example, "Military snipers use a **silencer** on their weapons so the enemy cannot detect their location."

Write a sentence using **silencer**.

_____

_____

3 A third meaning of **muffler** has no related words.

a. When **muffler** is used in this way, it means a <u>device inserted on a car exhaust to reduce noise</u>. For example, "Danny took the **muffler** off his hot rod because he thought a loud engine noise would make his car sound more powerful."

Write a sentence using **muffler**.

_____

_____

Word Meaning in Context

Muffler began in the Old French language as a word meaning "thick glove." Later, in the English language, this meaning expanded to include three current meanings:

- ❏ **article of clothing worn around the neck to keep warm**
- ❏ **device used to absorb sound**
- ❏ **device inserted on a car exhaust to reduce noise**

1. The **muffler** on my father's car has a hole in it, so you can hear him coming from two blocks away.

Which of the meanings of **muffler** is this? _____

_____

2. My neck was getting cold while I was sledding in the park, so my mother gave me a wool **muffler** to wear.

Which of the meanings of **muffler** is this? _____

_____

3. The engineers installed a **muffler** on all of the factory's machinery to protect the hearing of the workers.

Which of the meanings of **muffler** is this? _____

_____

Word Meaning Map   The teacher will give you the **Muffler** worksheet.

Complete Each Definition

1. **Muffler** can mean a scarf or article of clothing worn around the

_____ to keep warm.

2. **Muffler** can also mean a device, such as a muzzle or silencer, used to absorb

_____.

3. **Muffler** can also mean a device inserted on a _____
or automobile exhaust to reduce noise.

Understanding Check

Circle whether **muffler** is used as you would expect.

1. To help increase their performance, race cars do not have a **muffler** installed. When the drivers rev up their engines, the noise near the track is deafening.   Expect   Not Expect

2. The weather turned cold last night as the winter storm approached. My mother reminded me to wear a **muffler**, hat, and gloves if I was going to walk to school this morning.   Expect   Not Expect

3. My mother had her car tuned up last week. The mechanic changed the oil in her **muffler** and checked the air in her tires.   Expect   Not Expect

4. It has been raining heavily for the past few days. The streets are becoming so flooded that I had to wear a **muffler** over my shoes to keep them dry while walking through the puddles.   Expect   Not Expect

5. The newspaper's printing machine made a screeching noise that was causing headaches among the workers. The newspaper developed a **muffler** for the printing press that helped reduce the noise level and keep the workers healthy.   Expect   Not Expect

6. Many of the teachers complained they couldn't hear the fire alarm ring. The custodian needed to put a **muffler** onto the system to help the bell ring louder.   Expect   Not Expect

Create Stories

On a sheet of paper, write a short story or scenario for each of the three meanings of **muffler**.

Musical

Pre-Lesson Activity—Meanings of Related Words

1 One meaning of **musical** includes the following related words.

a. **Opera** can mean a <u>show that develops its story through songs</u>. For example, "My parents took me to an **opera** while we were vacationing in New York City."

Write a sentence using **opera**.

_____

_____

b. **Play** can mean a <u>show that develops its story through songs</u>. For example, "The **play** *Oliver* is about an orphan who grows up on the streets and steals to survive."

Write a sentence using **play**.

_____

_____

c. **Cabaret** can mean a <u>show that develops its story through songs</u>. For example, "The lead actress in the **cabaret** sang almost a dozen songs during the show."

Write a sentence using **cabaret**.

_____

_____

2 A second meaning of **musical** includes the following related words.

a. **Rhythmic** can mean a <u>characteristic of music</u>. For example, "When the flock of birds took off, the beating of their wings produced a **rhythmic** sound."

Write a sentence using **rhythmic**.

_____

_____

b. **Harmonious** can mean a <u>characteristic of music</u>. For example, "The Harlem Boy's Choir had a very **harmonious** sound throughout their concert."

Write a sentence using **harmonious**.

_____

_____

c. **Choral** can mean a <u>characteristic of music</u>. For example, "A group of sea lions was barking by the fishing pier in an almost **choral** tone, hoping the fishermen would throw them some fish."

Write a sentence using **choral**.

_____

_____

3 A third meaning of **musical** has no related words.

a. When **musical** is used in this way, it means to be <u>skilled in music</u>. For example, "Beethoven was an extremely **musical** child who had played in public since he was seven years old and had published music by the age of twelve."

Write a sentence using **musical**.

_____

_____

Word Meaning in Context

Musical began in the French language as a word meaning "musical party." Later, in the English language, this meaning expanded to include three current meanings:

- ❑ **show that develops its story through songs**
- ❑ **characteristic of music**
- ❑ **skilled in music**

1. Kristen is quite **musical** and can play several different instruments.

Which of the meanings of **musical** is this? _____

_____

2. The song "Tomorrow" is a popular song from the children's **musical** *Annie*.

Which of the meanings of **musical** is this? _____

_____

3. The radio disc jockey's voice has a **musical** quality that people enjoy listening to.

Which of the meanings of **musical** is this? _____

_____

Word Meaning Map   The teacher will give you the **Musical** worksheet.

Complete Each Definition

1. **Musical** can mean a movie or play that develops its story through

_____ or music.

2. **Musical** can also mean a characteristic or quality of _____
such as rhythm or harmony.

3. **Musical** can also mean to have a talent or be _____
in music.

Understanding Check

Circle whether **musical** is used as you would expect.

1. I have never been able to play the guitar or any other instrument. I consider myself to be very **musical**.   Expect   Not Expect

2. The Broadway play *Cats* contains several hit songs. The popularity of this **musical** helped make it the longest running show on Broadway.   Expect   Not Expect

3. John Lennon and Paul McCartney founded the legendary rock group called the Beatles. They were both very **musical** artists who wrote their own songs.   Expect   Not Expect

4. As the storm approached, the wind blew hard through the trees in the forest. The swaying branches and leaves made a **musical** sound.   Expect   Not Expect

5. My friends and I rented a horror movie the other night. It was a very scary **musical** about zombies and vampires.   Expect   Not Expect

6. I fell asleep in the basement last night and didn't hear a single noise all night long. The **musical** background noise helped me sleep like a baby.   Expect   Not Expect

Create Stories

On a sheet of paper, write a short story or scenario for each of the three meanings of **musical**.

Natural

Pre-Lesson Activity—Meanings of Related Words

1 One meaning of **natural** includes the following related words.

   a. **Normal** can mean <u>determined by nature's laws</u>. For example, "The doctor said my cold would follow its **normal** course, and that I should be feeling better within a few days."

   Write a sentence using **normal**.

   _____

   _____

   b. **Ordinary** can mean <u>determined by nature's laws</u>. For example, "In science class we studied the **ordinary** development of how a tadpole becomes a frog."

   Write a sentence using **ordinary**.

   _____

   _____

   c. **Usual** can mean <u>determined by nature's laws</u>. For example, "The **usual** weather pattern for Alaska during the month of December includes cold air and snow showers."

   Write a sentence using **usual**.

   _____

   _____

2 A second meaning of **natural** includes the following related words.

   a. **Intuitive** can mean <u>inborn</u>. For example, "For Wolfgang Amadeus Mozart, playing the piano seemed almost **intuitive**, since he had played professionally from a young age."

   Write a sentence using **intuitive**.

   _____

   _____

b. **Instinctive** can mean <u>inborn</u>. For example, "John had never played goalie before, but he blocked several shots in a very **instinctive** manner."

Write a sentence using **instinctive**.

_____

_____

c. **Innate** can mean <u>inborn</u>. For example, "Lilly always seemed to have an **innate** love for math."

Write a sentence using **innate**.

_____

_____

3 A third meaning of **natural** includes the following related words.

a. **Organic** can mean <u>not altered or treated</u>. For example, "My sister is very health conscious and will only buy **organic** foods."

Write a sentence using **organic**.

_____

_____

b. **Unrefined** can mean <u>not altered or treated</u>. For example, "**Unrefined** sugar is not bleached, so it has a darker appearance than refined sugar."

Write a sentence using **unrefined**.

_____

_____

c. **Genuine** can mean <u>not altered or treated</u>. For example, "The curl in my sister's hair is **genuine** and was not the result of a perm."

Write a sentence using **genuine**.

_____

_____

4 A fourth meaning of **natural** has no related words.

a. When **natural** is used in this way, it means to be <u>produced by nature</u>. For example, "Every Christmas my family argues about whether we will buy a **natural** tree or use the artificial one in the attic."

Write a sentence using **natural**.

_____

_____

Word Meaning in Context

Natural began in the Old French language as a word meaning "by birth." Later, in the English language, this meaning expanded to include four current meanings:

❑ **determined by nature's laws**
❑ **inborn**
❑ **not altered or treated**
❑ **produced by nature**

1. My mother was very excited when my father gave her a **natural** pearl necklace for their anniversary.

   Which of the meanings of **natural** is this? _____

   _____

2. The doctor said the old man died of **natural** causes.

   Which of the meanings of **natural** is this? _____

   _____

3. The doctor tapped my knee slightly while I was sitting down to see if my **natural** reflexes were okay.

   Which of the meanings of **natural** is this? _____

   _____

4. My mom buys **natural** flour, so it looks darker in color than flour that is bleached white.

   Which of the meanings of **natural** is this? _____

   _____

Word Meaning Map   The teacher will give you the **Natural** worksheet.

Complete Each Definition

1. **Natural** can mean organic or not altered or _____.

2. **Natural** can also mean to be determined by ordinary or _____ laws.

3. **Natural** can also mean innate or _____.

4. **Natural** can also mean to be present in or produced by _____.

Understanding Check

Circle whether **natural** is used as you would expect.

1. Susan has taken dozens of golf lessons, but she still can't seem to hit the ball very well. She thinks she has a **natural** ability for the game.

   Expect   Not Expect

2. Some expectant mothers prefer to deliver their babies at home rather than in a hospital. Nurses or midwives help these mothers with a **natural** childbirth.

   Expect   Not Expect

3. Our neighbor just bought a new Porsche 911 convertible sports car. He says it's one of the best **natural** products you can buy today.

   Expect   Not Expect

4. The oranges at the farmers market were fresh but didn't have a bright color to them. They were not dyed and had their **natural** coloring.

   Expect   Not Expect

5. The paramedics responded to the scene of an accident where a man was hit by a car. They tried providing medical care but said he died of **natural** causes.

   Expect   Not Expect

6. Leonard is one of the best athletes at our school. The P. E. teachers say he has **natural** athletic abilities.

   Expect   Not Expect

7. Most candies have refined or processed sugar that can be harmful to your teeth. This **natural** sugar promotes tooth decay.

   Expect   Not Expect

8. All of the plants in the principal's office are a shiny green color. Everyone who sees them asks the receptionist if they are **natural** or fake.

   Expect   Not Expect

Create Stories

On a sheet of paper, write a short story or scenario for each of the four meanings of **natural**.

The Multiple Meaning Vocabulary Program

Needle

Pre-Lesson Activity—Meanings of Related Words

1 One meaning of **needle** includes the following related words.

a. **Tease** can mean to <u>provoke by constantly criticizing</u>. For example, "Greg can be a bully sometimes, and he likes to **tease** younger kids."

Write a sentence using **tease**.

_____

_____

b. **Harass** can mean to <u>provoke by constantly criticizing</u>. For example, "Some of the younger students have complained that older students **harass** them in the schoolyard before school."

Write a sentence using **harass**.

_____

_____

c. **Pester** can mean to <u>provoke by constantly criticizing</u>. For example, "Sometimes I think my little brother's favorite hobby is to **pester** me."

Write a sentence using **pester**.

_____

_____

2 A second meaning of **needle** includes the following related words.

a. **Indicator** can mean a <u>pointer or dial on a scale</u>. For example, "The pilot looked at the altimeter's **indicator** to see how high above the ground she was flying."

Write a sentence using **indicator**.

_____

_____

b. **Cursor** can mean a <u>pointer or dial on a scale</u>. For example, "Some new cars have digital displays that use a **cursor** to show the car's speed."

Write a sentence using **cursor**.

_____

_____

c. **Arrow** can mean a <u>pointer or dial on a scale</u>. For example, "Our new thermometer has an **arrow** that points to the current temperature."

Write a sentence using **arrow**.

_____

_____

3 A third meaning of **needle** has no related words.

a. When **needle** is used in this way, it means a <u>sharp steel instrument that is pointed at one end</u>. For example, "My mother used a thread and **needle** to mend my torn pants."

Write a sentence using **needle**.

_____

_____

4 A fourth meaning of **needle** has no related words.

a. When **needle** is used in this way, it means a <u>sharp pointed object found in nature</u>. For example, "I was hiking in the Grand Canyon when I brushed against a cactus and got a **needle** stuck in my leg."

Write a sentence using **needle**.

_____

_____

Word Meaning in Context

Needle began in the Old English language as a word meaning "goad or provoke." Later, the meanings expanded to include four current meanings:

- ❑ **provoke by constantly criticizing**
- ❑ **pointer or dial on a scale**
- ❑ **sharp steel instrument that is pointed at one end**
- ❑ **sharp pointed object found in nature**

1. Julie doesn't enjoy hanging out with her younger brother, because he constantly tries to **needle** her.

Which of the meanings of **needle** is this?_____

_____

2. A compass **needle** will always point to magnetic north.

Which of the meanings of **needle** is this?_____

_____

3. The nurse gave all of the students the flu shot with a hypodermic **needle**.

Which of the meanings of **needle** is this?_____

_____

4. Jana brushed up against the dead pine tree and got a **needle** stuck in her coat.

Which of the meanings of **needle** is this?_____

_____

Word Meaning Map   The teacher will give you the **Needle** worksheet.

Complete Each Definition

1. Needle can mean to provoke or tease by _____
criticizing.

2. Needle can also mean a _____ or dial on scale
such a compass.

3. Needle can also mean a sharp steel instrument used for sewing or giving injections that is
_____ at one end.

4. Needle can also mean a sharp pointed object that is found in _____
_____ such as that found on a pine tree or cactus.

Understanding Check

Circle whether **needle** is used as you would expect.

1. My sister just got a new haircut and is not very happy with it. Now she doesn't want to go to school because she thinks her classmates will **needle** her about it.   Expect   Not Expect

2. Maple trees have broad flat leaves that change color in the fall. We like to find a different colored **needle** from each tree in our yard for our collection.   Expect   Not Expect

3. The pine tree belongs to the conifer family. This type of tree has a short green **needle** for a leaf.   Expect   Not Expect

4. My sister was nervous about singing in her first talent show at school. To help her relax we all tried to **needle** her about what a beautiful voice she has.   Expect   Not Expect

5. My mother said we needed to stop and get gas. I looked at the gas gauge and saw the **needle** was on empty.   Expect   Not Expect

6. The school nurse was recording everyone's height and weight for their sports physical. I stepped onto the **needle** and saw that I weighed 100 pounds.   Expect   Not Expect

7. I brought my new puppy to the veterinarian for its rabies shot. The doctor placed the **needle** into the scruff of the dog's neck.   Expect   Not Expect

8. My mom said she was going to knit me a new sweater for my birthday. She said the sweater would have to be red because that was the only colored **needle** she had left.   Expect   Not Expect

Create Stories

On a sheet of paper, write a short story or scenario for each of the four meanings of **needle**.

The Multiple Meaning Vocabulary Program

Notice

Pre-Lesson Activity—Meanings of Related Words

1 One meaning of **notice** includes the following related words.

  a. **Pay attention to** can mean to <u>become aware of</u>. For example, "Good teachers try to **pay attention to** all of their students."

    Write a sentence using **pay attention to**.

    _____

    _____

  b. **Observe** can mean to <u>become aware of</u>. For example, "Lifeguards are responsible for the safety of all swimmers and must quickly **observe** any person who might need assistance."

    Write a sentence using **observe**.

    _____

    _____

  c. **See** can mean to <u>become aware of</u>. For example, "The girl in the back of the classroom raised her hand so the teacher would **see** her."

    Write a sentence using **see**.

    _____

    _____

2 A second meaning of **notice** includes the following related words.

  a. **Review** can mean a <u>printed review of a play or movie</u>. For example, "The **review** of the new action movie said it was a waste of money."

    Write a sentence using **review**.

    _____

    _____

  b. **Critique** can mean a <u>printed review of a play or movie</u>. For example, "The **critique** of the Broadway musical said that it might win several Tony awards."

    Write a sentence using **critique**.

    _____

    _____

c. **Write up** can mean a <u>printed review of a play or movie</u>. For example, "I always read the **write up** on any movie I'm thinking of seeing so I don't end up wasting my time or money."

Write a sentence using **write up**.

_____

_____

3 A third meaning of **notice** includes the following related words.

a. **Bulletin** can mean a <u>written announcement</u>. For example, "The students posted a **bulletin** telling about the upcoming school dance."

Write a sentence using **bulletin**.

_____

_____

b. **Pamphlet** can mean a <u>written announcement</u>. For example, "The department store printed a **pamphlet** that listed what was on sale."

Write a sentence using **pamphlet**.

_____

_____

c. **Leaflet** can mean a <u>written announcement</u>. For example, "The **leaflet** posted on the side of the building gave information about a hip-hop artist who would be playing at the state fair this weekend."

Write a sentence using **leaflet**.

_____

_____

4 A fourth meaning of **notice** has no related words.

a. When **notice** is used in this way, it means the <u>condition of being formally warned</u>. For example, "The teacher gave **notice** to Michael that if he didn't perform better on the next math test, he might fail the course."

Write a sentence using **notice**.

_____

_____

Word Meaning in Context

Notice began in the Latin language as a word meaning "knowledge or fame." Later, in the English language, the meanings expanded to include four current meanings:

- ❑ **become aware of**
- ❑ **printed review of a play or movie**
- ❑ **written announcement**
- ❑ **condition of being formally warned**

1. Emily was sure everyone would **notice** that she spilt chocolate milk all over her shirt.

Which of the meanings of **notice** is this? _____

_____

2. The paper's **notice** of Disney's new movie was very flattering.

Which of the meanings of **notice** is this? _____

_____

3. The school custodian posted a **notice** stating that the bathrooms would be closed for several hours tomorrow due to maintenance.

Which of the meanings of **notice** is this? _____

_____

4. The coach gave the quarterback **notice** that if he didn't start playing better he would be benched.

Which of the meanings of **notice** is this? _____

_____

Word Meaning Map   The teacher will give you the **Notice** worksheet.

Complete Each Definition

1. **Notice** can mean to pay attention to or become _____

_____ of.

2. **Notice** can also mean a written or printed review of a _____ or movie.

3. **Notice** can also mean a pamphlet or other _____ announcement.

4. **Notice** can also mean a condition of being advised or formally _____.

Understanding Check

Circle whether **notice** is used as you would expect.

1. I forgot to do my math homework for class today. I spent most of the class crouching low in my seat so the teacher would **notice** me and ask me to do one of the problems on the board.

   Expect   Not Expect

2. I went to see the opening of the new Tom Cruise movie with my best friend Diana. We had to wait in line for a half hour before we could buy a **notice** to get into the theatre.

   Expect   Not Expect

3. The theater just started selling tickets for its new play. None of the critics have seen it yet, so the newspapers haven't published a **notice** for it.

   Expect   Not Expect

4. James scored an A+ on every math test this year. The teacher sat him down to give him **notice** about his performance.

   Expect   Not Expect

5. My boss was not very happy with my unwillingness to work on Saturday or Sunday. He gave me **notice** yesterday that unless I was willing to work on weekends, I would be fired.

   Expect   Not Expect

6. My father got a ticket for driving through a stop sign yesterday. He told the officer he never stopped because he did not **notice** the sign.

   Expect   Not Expect

7. The children's symphony will be playing in the park this Sunday afternoon. The members of the symphony made sure that every store downtown had a **notice** about the event posted in their window.

   Expect   Not Expect

8. Every morning, the principal talks to the school over the intercom. Today's **notice** concerned our upcoming holiday break.

   Expect   Not Expect

Create Stories

On a sheet of paper, write a short story or scenario for each of the four meanings of **notice**.

Pre-Lesson Activity—Meanings of Related Words

1 One meaning of **odd** includes the following related words.

   a. **Strange** can mean that someone or something is unusual and <u>different from what is expected</u>. For example, "Just before the thunderstorm came through the area, Brent noticed that his dog was acting **strange**."

   Write a sentence using **strange**.

   _____

   _____

   b. **Unusual** can mean that something does not happen very often and is <u>different from what is expected</u>. For example, "Cindy's teacher thought it was very **unusual** for her to do so poorly on a math test."

   Write a sentence using **unusual**.

   _____

   _____

   c. **Weird** can mean that someone or something is peculiar and <u>different from what is expected</u>. For example, "Allen felt the rock band's new CD was a bit **weird** compared to their previous CDs."

   Write a sentence using **weird**.

   _____

   _____

2 A second meaning of **odd** has no related words.

   a. When **odd** is used in this way, it means that a number <u>cannot be divided exactly by the number two</u> and is not even. For example, "Seven is an **odd** number."

   Write a sentence using **odd**.

   _____

   _____

3 A third meaning of **odd** includes the following related words.

    a. **Unmatched** means that something is without a corresponding mate and is <u>separated from its pair or set</u>. For example, "Alisha's mother had a drawer full of **unmatched** lids and bowls."

       Write a sentence using **unmatched**.

       _____

       _____

    b. **Remaining** can mean that something is left after things have been used or taken away and <u>separated from its pair or set</u>. For example, "The **remaining** cookie was being saved for the student who was at band practice during the class party."

       Write a sentence using **remaining**.

       _____

       _____

    c. **Single** can mean that something is not accompanied by another thing and is <u>separated from its pair or set</u>. For example, "When Max and Julio divided their grandfather's rock collection between them, they discovered that there was one **single** rock left over."

       Write a sentence using **single**.

       _____

       _____

4 A fourth meaning of **odd** includes the following related words.

    a. **Sporadic** can mean that something happens that is <u>not regular or planned</u>. For example, "Riley's summer job experiences were **sporadic**.

       Write a sentence using **sporadic**.

       _____

       _____

    b. **Occasional** can mean that something happens infrequently and is <u>not regular or planned</u>. For example, "Gina has the **occasional** habit of making noises with her mouth while working on the computer."

       Write a sentence using **occasional**.

       _____

       _____

    c. **Various** can mean that something happens at different times and is <u>not regular or planned</u>. For example, "We had **various** problems on our trip down the river, including being chased by an angry bear."

       Write a sentence using **various**.

       _____

       _____

Word Meaning in Context

Odd began in the Old German language as a word meaning "pointing upwards." Later, in the English language, this meaning changed and expanded to include four current meanings:

- ❑ **different from what is expected**
- ❑ **cannot be divided exactly by the number two**
- ❑ **separated from its pair or set**
- ❑ **not regular or planned**

1. Alexis earned extra money doing **odd** jobs in the neighborhood.

   Which of the meanings of **odd** is this? _____

   _____

2. The security guard noticed the **odd** behavior of the man before he robbed the bank.

   Which of the meanings of **odd** is this? _____

   _____

3. Pedro and his brother Marcos could not divide the candy evenly between them because they had an **odd** number of pieces.

   Which of the meanings of **odd** is this? _____

   _____

4. Reuben has a whole drawer full of **odd** socks.

   Which of the meanings of **odd** is this? _____

   _____

Word Meaning Map   The teacher will give you the **Odd** worksheet.

Complete Each Definition

1. **Odd** can mean that a number cannot be _____ exactly by the number two.

2. **Odd** can also mean that something is _____ from its pair or set.

3. **Odd** can also mean that something happens that is not _____ or planned, or does not occur very often.

4. **Odd** can also mean that something is strange and _____ from what is expected or customary.

Understanding Check

Circle whether **odd** is used as you would expect.

1. While searching for sea shells at the beach Lydia noticed one with a unique color and shape. She said to her mother, "What an **odd** shell."   Expect   Not Expect

2. Felicia observed that her volleyball team had an **odd** number of players at practice one afternoon. There were nine players present.   Expect   Not Expect

3. One winter morning before school, Craig looked through the box of **odd** gloves and mittens that was in the closet to see if he could find one of his missing gloves. Unfortunately, his glove was not there.   Expect   Not Expect

4. Bridget's father arrived home from work every day at the same time, which was 5:30 p.m. Bridget thought that her father got home from work at **odd** times.   Expect   Not Expect

5. Wyatt observed his friend Caleb put ketchup on his hot dog at lunch. Wyatt thought it was an **odd** thing to do because ketchup should not be placed on hot dogs.   Expect   Not Expect

6. Calvin's friend asked him, "Do you know you are wearing an **odd** pair of socks?" Calvin's socks were a perfect match and were exactly the same color.   Expect   Not Expect

7. One summer Tony worked at a lot of **odd** jobs in order to earn money to purchase an electric guitar. He painted houses, mowed lawns, and stocked shelves at a big discount store.   Expect   Not Expect

8. Jerry was eight years old, while his sisters, McKenzie and Zoe, were six and four years old, respectively. All of their ages were **odd** numbers.   Expect   Not Expect

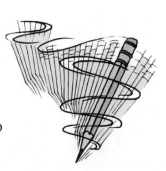

Create Stories

On a sheet of paper, write a short story or scenario for each of the four meanings of **odd**.

Operator

Pre-Lesson Activity—Meanings of Related Words

1 One meaning of **operator** includes the following related words.

a. **Receptionist** can mean <u>someone who works on a telephone switchboard</u>, often in a hotel, office, or hospital. For example, "Priscilla got a job at the new hotel in town as a **receptionist**, answering phones and dealing with people when they first arrive."

Write a sentence using **receptionist**.

_____

_____

b. **Secretary** can mean <u>someone who works on a telephone switchboard</u> and does office work. For example, "The **secretary** at the insurance office worked hard at such tasks as typing, filing, and answering the telephone."

Write a sentence using **secretary**.

_____

_____

c. **Administrative assistant** can mean <u>someone who works on a telephone switchboard</u> in an office and writes letters and arranges meetings. For example, "Karla's mother has been an **administrative assistant** at city hall for ten years."

Write a sentence using **administrative assistant**.

_____

_____

2 A second meaning of **operator** includes the following related words.

a. **Worker** can mean someone who <u>uses or controls a machine or vehicle</u>. For example, "Brady's father has a job as a **worker** on a large crane, a machine that is used to lift and move objects at construction sites."

Write a sentence using **worker**.

_____

_____

b. **Machinist** can mean someone who <u>uses or controls a machine</u>, especially in a factory. For example, "Jill works as a **machinist** in a clothing factory."

Write a sentence using **machinist**.

_____

_____

c. **Engineer** can mean someone who <u>uses or controls a machine or vehicle</u> or is in charge of an engine or locomotive. For example, "Larry gets to travel all over the country for his job as a train **engineer**." Write a sentence using **engineer**.

_____

_____

3 A third meaning of **operator** includes the following related words.

a. **Manager** can mean <u>someone who owns or runs a business</u> or other enterprise. For example, "Denise was told that the store **manager** does all the hiring." Write a sentence using **manager**.

_____

_____

b. **Proprietor** can mean <u>someone who owns or runs a business</u> or other such establishment. For example, "Raul's father is the **proprietor** of one of the best pizza places in the city." Write a sentence using **proprietor**.

_____

_____

c. **Boss** can mean <u>someone who owns or runs a business</u> or organization and supervises the work of others. For example, "The **boss** of the ice cream shop near McCalister Park is a kind elderly man who loves children." Write a sentence using **boss**.

_____

_____

4 A fourth meaning of **operator** includes the following related words.

a. **Manipulator** can mean someone who is a <u>shrewd person</u> and acts deceptively to improve his or her situation. For example, "The bully was a smooth manipulator who tricked Jasmin into helping him." Write a sentence using **manipulator**.

_____

_____

b. **Schemer** can mean someone who is a <u>shrewd person</u> and accomplishes his or her purposes by deceitful means. For example, "The man was such a clever **schemer** that he deceived many residents in the neighborhood." Write a sentence using **schemer**.

_____

_____

c. **Opportunist** can mean someone who is a <u>shrewd person</u> and takes advantage of situations in order to gain money or power. For example, "To the disappointment of everyone, the person who was elected mayor turned out to be an **opportunist**." Write a sentence using **opportunist**.

_____

_____

Word Meaning in Context

Operator began in the Latin language as a word meaning "to work." Later, in the English language, this meaning changed and expanded to include four current meanings:

- ❑ **someone who works on a telephone switchboard**
- ❑ **someone who uses or controls a machine or vehicle**
- ❑ **someone who owns or runs a business**
- ❑ **shrewd person**

1. Preston was a smooth **operator** when he tried to persuade Kevin to give him the cookies in his lunch.

Which of the meanings of **operator** is this? _____

_____

2. Rafael dialed the **operator** in order to make a long distance telephone call to his friend who lived in New York.

Which of the meanings of **operator** is this? _____

_____

3. Marisa's mother started a new job as a computer **operator** for an insurance company.

Which of the meanings of **operator** is this? _____

_____

4. The **operator** of the sandwich shop had been gone on vacation for two weeks.

Which of the meanings of **operator** is this? _____

_____

Word Meaning Map   The teacher will give you the **Operator** worksheet.

Complete Each Definition

1. **Operator** can mean someone who works on a _____

switchboard at a hotel, hospital, or other office environment.

2. **Operator** can also mean someone who operates, uses, or _____
a machine, vehicle, or device.

3. **Operator** can also mean someone who owns or _____
a business, industrial establishment, or enterprise.

4. **Operator** can also mean someone who is a _____
person who accomplishes his or her purposes by tricky means.

Understanding Check

Circle whether **operator** is used as you would expect.

1. Tori's grandmother enjoyed being an **operator** at the local hospital. Her job was to receive telephone calls and provide information and other assistance to telephone users.

   Expect   Not Expect

2. Carl got a job as a part-time custodian at the new fitness center and health club. Carl enjoyed being the **operator** of the business.

   Expect   Not Expect

3. Lacey was a mail carrier who delivered the mail to Emmanuel's house every afternoon. When Emmanuel grew up, he wanted to be a mail **operator** just like Lacey.

   Expect   Not Expect

4. Jimmy's father did not buy a used car from a neighbor down the street. This neighbor had a reputation as a smooth **operator** who was not trustworthy.

   Expect   Not Expect

5. Isabella's father was a computer **operator** for one of the largest insurance companies in the country. He enjoyed working on the computer.

   Expect   Not Expect

6. Hailey often visited a blind lady named Grace who lived near her house. Grace was a kind and trustworthy person. She was a smooth **operator**.

   Expect   Not Expect

7. Selena's aunt loves being a tour **operator**. She owns and runs a business that plans trips and vacations for people all over the world.

   Expect   Not Expect

8. Jeffrey was not very mechanical and did not know how to use or control any of the machines in the factory. He saw himself as a great **operator**.

   Expect   Not Expect

Create Stories

On a sheet of paper, write a short story or scenario for each of the four meanings of **operator**.

Pre-Lesson Activity—Meanings of Related Words

1 One meaning of **orbit** includes the following related words.

a. **Course** can mean the route or <u>curved path of an object, planet, or star as it travels in space</u>. For example, "Evelyn plotted the **course** of the moon for a science project."

Write a sentence using **course**.

_____

_____

b. **Track** can mean the direction or <u>curved path of an object, planet, or star as it travels in space</u>. For example, "The **track** of the spacecraft went around the planet Jupiter."

Write a sentence using **track**.

_____

_____

c. **Trajectory** can mean the <u>curved path of an object, planet, or star as it travels in space</u>. For example, "The engineers worked very hard to make sure that the **trajectory** of the spaceship was accurate and achievable."

Write a sentence using **trajectory**.

_____

_____

2 A second meaning of **orbit** includes the following related words.

a. **Sphere** can mean the <u>range of influence</u>, power, or control that a person, group, or nation has. For example, "The chess club was outside the **sphere** of the varsity football coach."

Write a sentence using **sphere**.

_____

_____

b. **Domain** can mean a <u>range of influence</u>. For example, "Lexie read about a king whose **domain** extended into three continents."

Write a sentence using **domain**.

_____

_____

c. **Field** can mean a <u>range of influence</u>. For example, "Laura's teacher was a leader in the **field** of mathematics."

Write a sentence using **field**.

_____

_____

3 A third meaning of **orbit** has no related words.

a. When **orbit** is used in this way, it means the <u>eye socket</u>, which is the bony cavity of the skull that contains the eyeball. For example, "Hayden required surgery on his right **orbit** because he was in a car accident."

Write a sentence using **orbit**.

_____

_____

Word Meaning in Context

Orbit began in the Latin language as a word meaning "circle and disc." Later, in the English language, the meanings expanded to include three current meanings:

- ❑ **curved path of an object, planet, or star as it travels in space**
- ❑ **range of influence**
- ❑ **eye socket**

1. On a field trip to the hospital, Cameron learned that the bony opening that encases each eyeball is called the **orbit**.

Which of the meanings of **orbit** is this? _____

_____

2. The satellite was launched into **orbit** around the moon.

Which of the meanings of **orbit** is this? _____

_____

3. The personality of the coach drew the new players into his **orbit**.

Which of the meanings of **orbit** is this? _____

_____

Word Meaning Map   The teacher will give you the **Orbit** worksheet.

Complete Each Definition

1. **Orbit** can mean a curved _____
of an object, planet, or star as it travels in space.

2. **Orbit** can also mean the bony cavity of the skull that contains the eyeball, which

is called the _____ socket.

3. **Orbit** can also mean the _____ of influence, control,
or knowledge of a person.

Understanding Check

Circle whether **orbit** is used as you would expect.

1. The communications satellite was launched into **orbit**. Jake
read about the satellite in his science magazine.   Expect   Not Expect

2. The horse trainer had an **orbit** that extended far beyond his
own ranch and herd of horses. He was well known throughout
the West.   Expect   Not Expect

3. Juan practiced hard and was a good swimmer. He swam into
orbit when he was swimming laps back and forth in the pool.   Expect   Not Expect

4. Adrian played baseball every afternoon after school. One day
he hurt his **orbit** when a baseball hit him in the eye.   Expect   Not Expect

5. During volleyball practice Rachel injured her **orbit**. The muscle
that connects her foot to her leg was sore for weeks.   Expect   Not Expect

6. No one was paying any attention to Franklin when he was
explaining the rules to a new game. Franklin drew all of the
other students into his **orbit** at recess.   Expect   Not Expect

Create Stories

On a sheet of paper, write a short story or scenario
for each of the three meanings of **orbit**.

Passage

Pre-Lesson Activity—Meanings of Related Words

1 One meaning of **passage** includes the following related words.

  a. **Citation** can mean a <u>section of written work</u>. For example, "Our English assignment was to recite a brief **citation** to the class from one of our favorite books."
Write a sentence using **citation**.

_____

_____

  b. **Quotation** can mean a <u>section of written work</u>. For example, "The history teacher read a **quotation** from Lincoln's Gettysburg address."
Write a sentence using **quotation**.

_____

_____

  c. **Excerpt** can mean a <u>section of written work</u>. For example, "To help get the class interested in the story, the teacher read a short **excerpt** from the next book we were about to start reading."
Write a sentence using **excerpt**.

_____

_____

2 A second meaning of **passage** includes the following related words.

  a. **Trek** can mean to <u>transition from one place or condition to another</u>. For example, "In 1909, the explorer Robert Peary and four Eskimos were the first people to make the **trek** to the North Pole."
Write a sentence using **trek**.

_____

_____

  b. **Transformation** can mean to <u>transition from one place or condition to another</u>. For example, "Kevin's voice has begun to change now that he has started his **transformation** into adulthood."
Write a sentence using **transformation**.

_____

_____

c. **Conversion** can mean to <u>transition from one place or condition to another</u>. For example, "The catepillar goes through a **conversion** within its cocoon prior to becoming a butterfly." Write a sentence using **conversion**.

_____

_____

3 A third meaning of **passage** includes the following related words.

a. **Road** can mean a <u>route a person travels</u>. For example, "The only **road** to the small village was washed out from the heavy rains." Write a sentence using **road**.

_____

_____

b. **Trail** can mean a <u>route a person travels</u>. For example, "The guide said the **trail** would lead us through the mountains to a small town on the other side."
Write a sentence using **trail**.

_____

_____

c. **Channel** can mean a <u>route a person travels</u>. For example, "The ship sailed through the narrow **channel** to get to the open ocean." Write a sentence using **channel**.

_____

_____

4 A fourth meaning of **passage** includes the following related words.

a. **Approval** can mean <u>authorization of a law by a legislative body</u>. For example, "The senate gave its **approval** of the bill by voting it into law."
Write a sentence using **approval**.

_____

_____

b. **Adoption** can mean <u>authorization of a law by a legislative body</u>. For example, "Parents and teachers asked their congressmen to support the **adoption** of an education bill that would provide more money to schools."
Write a sentence using **adoption**.

_____

_____

c. **Acceptance** can mean <u>authorization of a law by a legislative body</u>. For example, "The senator who sponsored the bill for universal health care hoped other senators would vote for its **acceptance**." Write a sentence using **acceptance**.

_____

_____

Word Meaning in Context

Passage began in the Old French language as a word meaning "to go by." Later, in the English language, this meaning expanded to include four current meanings:

- ❏ **section of written work**
- ❏ **transition from one place or condition to another**
- ❏ **route a person travels**
- ❏ **authorization of a law by a legislative body**

1. The young man read a **passage** from a poem to his girlfriend.

Which of the meanings of **passage** is this? _____

_____

2. The **passage** from elementary to high school is a major event for many students.

Which of the meanings of **passage** is this? _____

_____

3. Heavy snowfall during the winter can block the **passage** to our cabin in the mountains.

Which of the meanings of **passage** is this? _____

_____

4. Britain's **passage** of the Stamp Act in 1765 to collect money from the American colonists led to large-scale protests and rioting.

Which of the meanings of **passage** is this? _____

_____

Word Meaning Map   The teacher will give you the **Passage** worksheet.

Complete Each Definition

1. **Passage** can mean an excerpt or _____ of written work.

2. **Passage** can also mean a trek or _____ from one place or condition to another.

3. **Passage** can also mean a road or _____ a person travels.

4. **Passage** can also mean the adoption or authorization of a _____ by a legislative body.

Understanding Check

Circle whether **passage** is used as you would expect.

1. Cindy really enjoyed reading Shakespeare's play *Romeo and Juliet*. Her favorite **passage** was when Romeo visits Juliet at her balcony.

   Expect   Not Expect

2. My father told my older sister to enjoy her time at college. He told her that for many people college is the final **passage** into adulthood.

   Expect   Not Expect

3. The president said he supported the bill for decreasing taxes. The president asked Americans to call their congressmen to ensure the **passage** of the bill.

   Expect   Not Expect

4. Many of the Mayan ruins in Mexico were found only recently. The **passage** through dense jungle growth kept people from finding these ancient cities.

   Expect   Not Expect

5. The teacher showed the class a black-and-white picture of President Teddy Roosevelt. The **passage** was taken in 1901 when, at the age of 42, he became the twenty-sixth president of the United States.

   Expect   Not Expect

6. On the cruise ship, the restaurants were all located on the third deck. The main **passage** led to each of the ship's dining areas.

   Expect   Not Expect

7. The senate voted down a bill to raise personal income taxes. The **passage** of this bill was no surprise because a survey showed most Americans disapproved of the bill.

   Expect   Not Expect

8. The captain anchored the boat in the harbor to minimize damage from the approaching hurricane. The boat made safe **passage** with several other ships tied down next to her.

   Expect   Not Expect

Create Stories

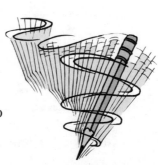

On a sheet of paper, write a short story or scenario for each of the four meanings of **passage**.

TARGET WORD | # Patient

Pre-Lesson Activity—Meanings of Related Words

1 One meaning of **patient** includes the following related words.

    a. **Sick person** can mean a <u>person under medical care</u>. For example, "The doctor gave medication to the **sick person** to help her recover from the flu."

       Write a sentence using **sick person**.

       _____

       _____

    b. **Invalid** can mean a <u>person under medical care</u>. For example, "The paramedics carried the **invalid** from the ambulance into the emergency room."

       Write a sentence using **invalid**.

       _____

       _____

    c. **Case** can mean a <u>person under medical care</u>. For example, "The doctor's next **case** was waiting in the emergency room."

       Write a sentence using **case**.

       _____

       _____

2 A second meaning of **patient** includes the following related words.

    a. **Composed** can mean <u>calm or even tempered</u>. For example, "The young boy was **composed**, even though he was lost in the big city."

       Write a sentence using **composed**.

       _____

       _____

b. **Easygoing** can mean <u>calm or even tempered</u>. For example, "My cousin is a professional surfer from California and has a very **easygoing** personality."

Write a sentence using **easygoing**.

_____

_____

c. **Gentle** can mean <u>calm or even tempered</u>. For example, "Mrs. Walker is my favorite teacher because she has a very **gentle** way with people."

Write a sentence using **gentle**.

_____

_____

3 A third meaning of **patient** includes the following related words.

a. **Uncomplaining** can mean <u>capable of bearing pain and suffering</u>. For example, "My grandfather is very tough and **uncomplaining**, even when his arthritis causes him to be in pain."

Write a sentence using **uncomplaining**.

_____

_____

b. **Enduring** can mean <u>capable of bearing pain and suffering</u>. For example, "The marathon runner was **enduring** the race, even after she twisted her ankle."

Write a sentence using **enduring**.

_____

_____

c. **Untiring** can mean <u>capable of bearing pain and suffering</u>. For example, "Our dog Molly was **untiring** while she gave birth to a litter of eight puppies."

Write a sentence using **untiring**.

_____

_____

Word Meaning in Context

Patient began in the Old French language as a word meaning "to suffer or endure." Later, in the English language, the meanings expanded to include three current meanings:

- ❑ **person under medical care**
- ❑ **calm or even tempered**
- ❑ **capable of bearing pain and suffering**

1. The **patient** was being prepared for an operation to remove his tonsils.

Which of the meanings of **patient** is this? _____

_____

2. I find it difficult to be **patient** when someone is hurrying me.

Which of the meanings of **patient** is this? _____

_____

3. My brother is very **patient** about not scratching himself despite having a bad case of poison ivy.

Which of the meanings of **patient** is this? _____

_____

Word Meaning Map   The teacher will give you the **Patient** worksheet.

Complete Each Definition

1. **Patient** can mean a sick person or someone under _____ care.

2. **Patient** can also mean being easygoing, _____ , or even tempered.

3. **Patient** can also mean uncomplaining or capable of bearing _____ or suffering.

The Multiple Meaning Vocabulary Program

Understanding Check

Circle whether **patient** is used as you would expect.

1. The highway was jammed with traffic this morning during rush hour. Everyone was very **patient**, honking horns and screaming at each other.

   Expect   Not Expect

2. The doctor was worried about one of the **patients** in the children's ward. The **patient** had been running a very high fever for several days.

   Expect   Not Expect

3. Charlie has been very **patient** with having the flu. He spent most of last night screaming and crying every time his mother left him alone.

   Expect   Not Expect

4. The best thing about my dad is that he is always very **patient** with me. Even if I make a mistake, he doesn't scream or get angry with me.

   Expect   Not Expect

5. The doctor needed to take the boy's temperature to see if he was still running a fever. He placed a small **patient** in the boy's mouth for one minute and saw that it was reading normal at 98.6 degrees.

   Expect   Not Expect

6. My grandmother has been very **patient** with her broken hip. It hurts her to sit up, but she always smiles and asks how everyone is doing.

   Expect   Not Expect

Create Stories

On a sheet of paper, write a short story or scenario for each of the three meanings of **patient**.

Pledge

Pre-Lesson Activity—Meanings of Related Words

1 One meaning of **pledge** includes the following related words.

a. **Vow** can mean a <u>promise to do something</u>. For example, "Many religious leaders, including Buddhist monks, take a **vow** to live a life of poverty."

Write a sentence using **vow**.

_____

_____

b. **Oath** can mean a <u>promise to do something</u>. For example, "When physicians graduate from medical school they take the Hippocratic **oath** to help others."

Write a sentence using **oath**.

_____

_____

c. **Word of honor** can mean a <u>promise to do something</u>. For example, "In a court of law, everyone who testifies must give their **word of honor** that they will tell the truth."

Write a sentence using **word of honor**.

_____

_____

2 A second meaning of **pledge** includes the following related words.

a. **Collateral** can mean <u>something held to ensure payment of a debt</u>. For example, "The man used his gold watch as **collateral** for the money he borrowed from a pawn shop."

Write a sentence using **collateral**.

_____

_____

b. **Guarantee** can mean <u>something held to ensure payment of a debt</u>. For example, "The banker wanted a **guarantee** from the young man before he would give him a loan."

Write a sentence using **guarantee**.

_____

_____

c. **Security** can mean <u>something held to ensure payment of a debt</u>. For example, "My parents needed to leave their credit card number as **security** before they could rent a car." Write a sentence using **security**.

_____

_____

3 A third meaning of **pledge** includes the following related words.

a. **Tribute** can mean <u>toast or drink a toast to</u>. For example, "The father of the bride raised a glass of champagne to make a **tribute** to his daughter on the day of her wedding." Write a sentence using **tribute**.

_____

_____

b. **Salute** can mean <u>toast or drink a toast to</u>. For example, "All of the players raised their cups of sports drink to **salute** their coach after winning the championship." Write a sentence using **salute**.

_____

_____

c. **Greeting** can mean <u>toast or drink a toast to</u>. For example, "Jenny's best friend gave Jenny a formal **greeting** as she arrived at her birthday party." Write a sentence using **greeting**.

_____

_____

4 A fourth meaning of **pledge** includes the following related words.

a. **Initiate** means <u>a person who promises to join a fraternity or sorority</u>. For example, "The college fraternity made every new **initiate** wear a tie and jacket to dinner every night for a week." Write a sentence using **initiate**.

_____

_____

b. **New member** can mean a <u>person who promises to join a fraternity or sorority</u>. For example, "My brother went to college and became a **new member** of the same fraternity my father belonged to when he was in school." Write a sentence using **new member**.

_____

_____

c. **Candidate** can mean a <u>person who promises to join a fraternity or sorority</u>. For example, "Prior to becoming a member of the fraternity, everyone must be a **candidate** for several months." Write a sentence using **candidate**.

_____

_____

Word Meaning in Context

Pledge began in the Old French language as a word meaning "bail or security." Later, in the English language, the meanings expanded to include four current meanings:

- ❏ **promise to do something**
- ❏ **something held to ensure a payment of debt**
- ❏ **toast or drink a toast to**
- ❏ **person who promises to join a fraternity or sorority**

1. Girl Scouts make a **pledge** to be honest and trustworthy.

Which of the meanings of **pledge** is this?_____

_____

2. The man used his house as a **pledge** for a new loan.

Which of the meanings of **pledge** is this?_____

_____

3. On New Year's Eve, it's common to raise a drink and **pledge** to everyone's happiness.

Which of the meanings of **pledge** is this?_____

_____

4. The college fraternities have an open house so anyone interested in becoming a **pledge** can meet the fraternity's members.

Which of the meanings of **pledge** is this?_____

_____

Word Meaning Map   The teacher will give you the **Pledge** worksheet.

Complete Each Definition

1. **Pledge** can mean something held such as collateral to ensure _____

_____ of a debt.

2. **Pledge** can also mean to toast or _____ a toast to.

3. **Pledge** can also mean a person who pledges to join a _____ or sorority.

4. **Pledge** can also mean a vow or _____ to do something.

Understanding Check

Circle whether **pledge** is used as you would expect.

1. My father was very upset with our mayor, who is running for re-election. He stood up to yell a **pledge** at him for breaking the promises he made during the last election.

   Expect   Not Expect

2. John's brother just graduated from the police academy. Once he received his badge, he made a **pledge** to uphold the law.

   Expect   Not Expect

3. We went snorkeling on our vacation in Hawaii. We had to leave our car keys as a **pledge** to return the equipment we rented.

   Expect   Not Expect

4. My dad did not need to borrow money from the bank to build our summer house. He needed to establish a **pledge** with the bank to get a home loan.

   Expect   Not Expect

5. Cindy told her friend Sheryl that she was not sure she would be able to come to her birthday party. When she didn't make it, Sheryl wasn't upset because she remembered the **pledge** she gave her.

   Expect   Not Expect

6. The president of the fraternity is a senior who has been a member for almost four years. He is now the most senior **pledge** in the house.

   Expect   Not Expect

7. The school's marching band won the state championship last week. After the competition, the band members raised their glasses of soda and made a **pledge** to the director to thank him for all his hard work.

   Expect   Not Expect

8. My best friend wants me to join his fraternity. I'm not sure if I want to be treated like a **pledge** though.

   Expect   Not Expect

Create Stories

On a sheet of paper, write a short story or scenario for each of the four meanings of **pledge**.

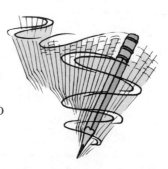

 **Plow**

Pre-Lesson Activity—Meanings of Related Words

1 One meaning of **plow** includes the following related words.

   a. **Till** can mean to <u>turn up soil</u>. For example, "The farmer got up at dawn so he could **till** his fields."

      Write a sentence using **till**.

      _____

      _____

   b. **Cultivate** can mean to <u>turn up soil</u>. For example, "Every spring, farmers **cultivate** their fields so they can plant new crops."

      Write a sentence using **cultivate**.

      _____

      _____

   c. **Break ground** can mean to <u>turn up soil</u>. For example, "The farmers were afraid a late snowfall would not allow them to **break ground** and seed their fields."

      Write a sentence using **break ground**.

      _____

      _____

2 A second meaning of **plow** includes the following related words.

   a. **Push** can mean <u>move forcefully through something</u>. For example, "My brother said he was going to stay up late tonight and **push** through a lot of his homework assignments."

      Write a sentence using **push**.

      _____

      _____

c. **Slam** can mean <u>move forcefully through something</u>. For example, "A defensive lineman's job is to **slam** through the offensive line and tackle the quarterback or running back."

Write a sentence using **slam**.

_____

_____

d. **Smash** can mean <u>move forcefully through something</u>. For example, "The cavalry tried to **smash** through the enemy's defenses."

Write a sentence using **smash**.

_____

_____

3 A third meaning of **plow** has no related words.

a. When **plow** is used in this way, it means a <u>heavy bladed instrument used to move dirt or snow</u>. For example, "Early settlers used horses to pull a heavy metal **plow** through their fields to ready them for planting."

Write a sentence using **plow**.

_____

_____

Word Meaning in Context

Plow began in the Old English language as a word meaning "a measure of land." Later, this meaning expanded to include three current meanings:

- ❏ **turn up soil**
- ❏ **move forcefully through something**
- ❏ **heavy bladed instrument used to move dirt or snow**

1. Some farmers in many third-world countries still use oxen to **plow** their fields.

Which of the meanings of **plow** is this? _____

_____

2. I was watching an action movie where the bank robbers tried to **plow** their car through a police barricade.

Which of the meanings of **plow** is this? _____

_____

3. My cousin lives in the Rocky Mountains and has a snow **plow** on his truck to make sure he never gets stuck in a blizzard.

Which of the meanings of **plow** is this? _____

_____

Word Meaning Map   The teacher will give you the **Plow** worksheet.

Complete Each Definition

1. **Plow** can mean to till or turn up _____.

2. **Plow** can also mean to push or move _____
through something.

3. **Plow** can also mean a heavy _____ instrument used to move dirt or snow.

Understanding Check

Circle whether **plow** is used as you would expect.

1. The tractor broke down in the middle of the cornfield. The farmer needed to take the **plow** off the broken tractor and put it on one that worked so he could finish tilling the field.   Expect   Not Expect

2. My sister wanted to see her favorite rock group in concert. When the theater opened its doors to sell tickets, she tried to **plow** through the crowd to be first in line at the ticket booth.   Expect   Not Expect

3. During the Depression, some poor sharecroppers would **plow** their fields without the use of animals. These farmers were too poor to own an animal or tractor.   Expect   Not Expect

4. Crop dusters are airplanes that fly over farms and spray crops. These planes have provided farmers a cheap and efficient way to **plow** their fields.   Expect   Not Expect

5. The freezing rain left the city's streets covered with ice. To prevent accidents on the roads, the city said that each car needed to put on a **plow** for safety's sake.   Expect   Not Expect

6. Our baby kitten isn't strong enough to push open the cat door to get into the house. It's fun to watch her **plow** through the door, but it doesn't even move.   Expect   Not Expect

Create Stories

On a sheet of paper, write a short story or scenario for each of the three meanings of **plow**.

Quarrel

Pre-Lesson Activity—Meanings of Related Words

1 One meaning of **quarrel** includes the following related words.

   a. **Dispute** can mean a <u>disagreement or to find fault with</u>. For example, "The couple in the video store had a **dispute** about what video they were going to rent."

   Write a sentence using **dispute**.

   _____

   _____

   b. **Bicker** can mean a <u>disagreement or to find fault with</u>. For example, "After several hours of traveling, everyone in the car started to **bicker** with each other."

   Write a sentence using **bicker**.

   _____

   _____

   c. **Criticize** can mean <u>disagreement or to find fault with</u>. For example, "The parents called the board of education to **criticize** the principal's decision to drop the music program."

   Write a sentence using **criticize**.

   _____

   _____

2 A second meaning of **quarrel** includes the following related words.

   a. **Shaft** can mean <u>arrow shot from a crossbow</u>. For example, "Part of being a good archer during ancient times was the ability to make a good **shaft** that would fly true."

   Write a sentence using **shaft**.

   _____

   _____

b. **Bolt** can mean <u>arrow shot from a crossbow</u>. For example, "The **bolt** flew out of the crossbow once the archer pulled the trigger."

Write a sentence using **bolt**.

_____

_____

c. **Dart** can mean <u>arrow shot from a crossbow</u>. For example, "The archers practiced shooting a **dart** at the center of the target."

Write a sentence using **dart**.

_____

_____

3 A third meaning of **quarrel** has no related words.

a. When **quarrel** is used in this way, it means <u>tool used for cutting stone</u>. For example, "A **quarrel** has a diamond tip to help it cut through stone."

Write a sentence using **quarrel**.

_____

_____

Word Meaning in Context

Quarrel began in the Old French language as a word meaning "square."
Later, in the English language, this meaning changed and expanded
to include three current meanings:

- ❏ **disagreement or to find fault with**
- ❏ **arrow shot from a crossbow**
- ❏ **tool used for cutting stone**

1. The mason used a **quarrel** to cut the tiles for the kitchen.

Which of the meanings of **quarrel** is this? _____

_____

2. My parents were complaining that my sister and I constantly **quarrel** with each other.

Which of the meanings of **quarrel** is this? _____

_____

3. Soldiers during the Middle Ages used shields and heavy armor to protect themselves from
being injured by a sword or **quarrel**.

Which of the meanings of **quarrel** is this? _____

_____

Word Meaning Map   The teacher will give you the **Quarrel** worksheet.

Complete Each Definition

1. **Quarrel** can mean a _____ or dispute, or
to find fault with.

2. **Quarrel** can also mean a bolt or _____ shot from
a crossbow.

3. **Quarrel** can also mean a device or _____ used to
cut stone.

Understanding Check

Circle whether **quarrel** is used as you would expect.

1. The guidance counselor told our class that we should listen to people who have different views than our own. She said that just because people have different beliefs, they don't need to **quarrel**.

   Expect   Not Expect

2. The Roman soldier drew his sword when the stranger approached the gate the soldier was guarding. Once the man identified himself, the soldier placed his sword back into its **quarrel**.

   Expect   Not Expect

3. The bridge was made from giant stones brought in from a rock quarry. The stones were cut with a **quarrel**, then shipped by train.

   Expect   Not Expect

4. My parents said we would be vacationing at Disneyland this year. My brother and I both had a **quarrel** with the idea because we always wanted to go there.

   Expect   Not Expect

5. Archers stood guard on top of the castle walls. They were supposed to shoot any enemy soldiers with a **quarrel** if they approached the castle.

   Expect   Not Expect

6. The science teacher was holding a paper airplane competition for his students. He told the students to grab a **quarrel** and cut up a sheet of construction paper to make an airplane.

   Expect   Not Expect

Create Stories

On a sheet of paper, write a short story or scenario for each of the three meanings of **quarrel**.

TARGET WORD | Quarter

Pre-Lesson Activity—Meanings of Related Words

1 One meaning of **quarter** includes the following related words.

    a. **District** can mean a <u>specific area of a city</u>. For example, "Midtown is the business **district** of Manhattan, where most of the skyscrapers are located."
Write a sentence using **district**.

_____

_____

    b. **Neighborhood** can mean a <u>specific area of a city</u>. For example, "My grandpa lives in New York, and he swears that the best Italian restaurants are located in a **neighborhood** called Little Italy."
Write a sentence using **neighborhood**.

_____

_____

    c. **Province** can mean a <u>specific area of a city</u>. For example, "In the French **province** of Quebec, many of the street signs are in French."
Write a sentence using **province**.

_____

_____

2 A second meaning of **quarter** includes the following related words.

    a. **Kindness** can mean <u>mercy given to an enemy</u>. For example, "During the Gulf War, millions of pamphlets were dropped to the Iraqi soldiers, telling them that they would be offered safety and **kindness** if they surrendered."
Write a sentence using **kindness**.

_____

_____

    b. **Compassion** can mean <u>mercy given to an enemy</u>. For example, "Every country that signed the Geneva Convention pact agreed to show **compassion** to enemy soldiers that were captured during war."
Write a sentence using **compassion**.

_____

_____

c. **Leniency** can mean <u>mercy given to an enemy</u>. For example, "Enemy soldiers are more likely to surrender if they know they will be shown **leniency**."
Write a sentence using **leniency**.

_____

_____

3 A third meaning of **quarter** includes the following related words.

a. **One fourth** can mean <u>one of four equal parts</u>. For example, "My father gives me **one fourth** of my monthly allowance every Friday."
Write a sentence using **one fourth**.

_____

_____

b. **Portion** can mean <u>one of four equal parts</u>. For example, "My mother gave everyone a **portion** of the apple pie she baked."
Write a sentence using **portion**.

_____

_____

c. **Piece** can mean <u>one of four equal parts</u>. For example, "Jane's three friends gave her an equal **piece** of the prize."
Write a sentence using **piece**.

_____

_____

4 A fourth meaning of **quarter** includes the following related words.

a. **Lodge** can mean to <u>provide housing</u>. For example, "The Red Cross was looking for families that could **lodge** people who lost their homes from the tornado."
Write a sentence using **lodge**.

_____

_____

b. **Board** can mean to <u>provide housing</u>. For example, "My brother is applying to colleges that can **board** students on campus."
Write a sentence using **board**.

_____

_____

c. **House** can mean to <u>provide housing</u>. For example, "The scout leader was hoping there would be enough cabins to **house** all of the scouts coming to the jamboree."
Write a sentence using **house**.

_____

_____

Word Meaning in Context

Quarter began in the Old French language as a word meaning "fourth part." Later, in the English language, this meaning expanded to include four current meanings:

- ❏ specific area of a city
- ❏ mercy given to an enemy
- ❏ one of four equal parts
- ❏ provide housing

1. The army set up tents in the fields to **quarter** all of the soldiers.

   Which of the meanings of **quarter** is this? _____

   _____

2. The French **Quarter** is where the celebration of Mardis Gras is held in New Orleans.

   Which of the meanings of **quarter** is this? _____

   _____

3. When the Roman Empire was at its peak, **quarter** was rarely given to anyone who rebelled against the emperor.

   Which of the meanings of **quarter** is this? _____

   _____

4. Since there were four of us sharing the pizza, everyone ate a **quarter** of the pie.

   Which of the meanings of **quarter** is this? _____

   _____

Word Meaning Map   The teacher will give you the **Quarter** worksheet.

Complete Each Definition

1. **Quarter** can mean a neighborhood or specific area of a _____

   _____.

2. **Quarter** can also mean kindness or mercy given to an _____.

3. **Quarter** can also mean a portion or one of _____ equal parts.

4. **Quarter** can also mean to lodge or provide _____.

Understanding Check

Circle whether **quarter** is used as you would expect.

1. The city of Savannah in Georgia was one of the first planned cities in the United States. The city's historic **quarter** was designed around numerous squares or small parks.   Expect   Not Expect

2. During World War II, the Russian army treated German prisoners of war with cruelty, sentencing many of them to labor camps. The Russians granted the prisoners **quarter** since Germany had invaded their country.   Expect   Not Expect

3. I only had 75 cents in my pocket but wanted to buy a candy bar that cost one dollar. I told my friend that if he gave me 25 cents, I would give a **quarter** of the candy bar to him.   Expect   Not Expect

4. California is a very large state. The **quarter** has several cities with over a million people including Los Angeles, San Diego, and San Francisco.   Expect   Not Expect

5. The Roman soldiers built a large ramp to attack the Jewish fort of Massadah that sat on top of a mountain. It is believed that the Romans refused to grant **quarter** to any of the Jewish soldiers or families inside.   Expect   Not Expect

6. My brother and I ate an entire pizza last night. After we split the pie in two, we each ate our **quarter** watching the football game.   Expect   Not Expect

7. George Washington's army survived a long winter at Valley Forge with few supplies. During this time period it was common for armies to stop fighting and take up winter **quarter** during the coldest months.   Expect   Not Expect

8. Our neighbor lost his job and could no longer pay his rent. The landlord gave him **quarter** and made him move out of the apartment.   Expect   Not Expect

Create Stories

On a sheet of paper, write a short story or scenario for each of the four meanings of **quarter**.

Queen

Pre-Lesson Activity—Meanings of Related Words

1 One meaning of **queen** includes the following related words.

   a. **Empress** can mean a <u>female ruler</u>. For example, "Cleopatra became the **empress** of Egypt when she was only 17 years old."

     Write a sentence using **empress**.

     _____

     _____

   b. **Monarch** can mean a <u>female ruler</u>. For example, "The young woman married the king and became a **monarch**."

     Write a sentence using **monarch**.

     _____

     _____

   c. **Sovereign** can mean a <u>female ruler</u>. For example, "A coronation is the celebration when the **sovereign** receives her royal throne."

     Write a sentence using **sovereign**.

     _____

     _____

2 A second meaning of **queen** includes the following related words.

   a. **Feline** can mean a <u>female cat used for breeding</u>. For example, "Buying kittens from a **feline** that is a rare breed can cost a lot of money."

     Write a sentence using **feline**.

     _____

     _____

3 A third meaning of **queen** has no related words.

    a. When **queen** is used in this way, it means a <u>female bee, ant, or termite that can lay eggs</u>. For example, "There is only one **queen** in a honey bee colony."

       Write a sentence using **queen**.

       _____

       _____

4 A fourth meaning of **queen** has no related words.

    a. When **queen** is used in this way, it means a <u>valuable game piece used in chess or cards</u>. For example, "In chess, the **queen** has more options for moving around the game board than any other piece."

       Write a sentence using **queen**.

       _____

       _____

Word Meaning in Context

Queen began in the Old English language as a word meaning "honored woman." Later, this meaning expanded to include four current meanings:

- ❑ **female ruler**
- ❑ **female cat used for breeding**
- ❑ **female bee, ant, or termite that can lay eggs**
- ❑ **valuable game piece used in chess or cards**

1. Grace won the game of blackjack when she was dealt a **queen** and an ace.

    Which of the meanings of **queen** is this? _____

    _____

2. **Queen** Elizabeth is the head of the royal family in England.

    Which of the meanings of **queen** is this? _____

    _____

3. My mother is hoping our little kitten will be pretty enough to be used as a **queen** when she gets older.

Which of the meanings of **queen** is this? _____

_____

4. The **queen** of an African termite colony can reach a length of 5 inches and lay as many as 30,000 eggs in a day.

Which of the meanings of **queen** is this? _____

_____

Word Meaning Map   The teacher will give you the **Queen** worksheet.

Complete Each Definition

1. **Queen** can mean a monarch or _____ ruler.

2. **Queen** can also mean a female _____ used for breeding.

3. **Queen** can also mean a valuable _____ piece that is used in chess or cards.

4. **Queen** can also mean a female bee, ant, or termite that can lay _____ for reproduction.

Understanding Check

Circle whether **queen** is used as you would expect.

1. My sister has a large male cat named Rudy. She hopes to use him as a **queen** for breeding. Expect   Not Expect

2. I was playing cards and only needed one more card for a royal flush. I was hoping my next card was going to be the **queen** of diamonds. Expect   Not Expect

3. The majority of all bees in a colony are male and make wax and feed larvae. These **queen** bees work very hard to build and maintain the colony. Expect   Not Expect

4. In chess, the piece shaped like a horse is called the **queen**. This game piece moves only in the shape of the letter L. Expect   Not Expect

5. **Queen** Isabella I of Spain funded Christopher Columbus' voyage to try and find a new route to India in 1492. She gave him money to make the voyage with 87 men and three ships, called the Niña, the Pinta, and the Santa Maria. Expect   Not Expect

6. When a colony of bees becomes too crowded, the bees will begin to swarm. This is when part of the colony flies off with the old **queen** to find a new home. Expect   Not Expect

7. Prince William is a possible heir to the British throne. This means that someday he may become the **queen**. Expect   Not Expect

8. My mom's American Bobtail cat has won several local pet shows. All of the neighbors have told her they would buy a kitten from one of her litters, if my mom decides to make her a **queen**. Expect   Not Expect

Create Stories

On a sheet of paper, write a short story or scenario for each of the four meanings of **queen**.

Pre-Lesson Activity—Meanings of Related Words

1 One meaning of **quiz** includes the following related words.

a. **Interrogate** can mean to <u>question repeatedly</u>. For example, "The FBI was sending in a special agent to **interrogate** the witnesses about the bank robbery."

Write a sentence using **interrogate**.

_____

_____

b. **Cross-examine** can mean to <u>question repeatedly</u>. For example, "The attorney knew she could prove the witness was lying once she was allowed to **cross-examine** him."

Write a sentence using **cross-examine**.

_____

_____

c. **Pump** can mean to <u>question repeatedly</u>. For example, "Julie's friends tried to **pump** her for information about how her date went last night."

Write a sentence using **pump**.

_____

_____

2 A second meaning of **quiz** includes the following related words.

a. **Hoax** can mean a <u>practical joke</u>. For example, "On Halloween, my brother and I always try to pull a **hoax** on our neighbors."

Write a sentence using **hoax**.

_____

_____

b. **Trick** can mean a <u>practical joke</u>. For example, "The class tried to pull a **trick** on the teacher by constantly setting the classroom clock back throughout the day."

Write a sentence using **trick**.

_____

_____

c. **Prank** can mean a <u>practical joke</u>. For example, "My best friend is always trying to pull a **prank** on his little sister."
Write a sentence using **prank**.

_____

_____

3 A third meaning of **quiz** includes the following related words.

a. **Probe** can mean a <u>short written test</u>. For example, "Our teacher always asks new students to take a quick math **probe** to determine the math level they will start at."
Write a sentence using **probe**.

_____

_____

b. **Exam** can mean <u>short written test</u>. For example, "I forgot we were having a spelling **exam** today, so I had to study during recess."
Write a sentence using **exam**.

_____

_____

c. **Evaluation** can mean <u>short written test</u>. For example, "At the end of each chapter in our social studies text is a ten-question **evaluation** of what was just covered."
Write a sentence using **evaluation**.

_____

_____

4 A fourth meaning of **quiz** includes the following related words.

a. **Tease** can mean to <u>make fun of</u>. For example, "My sister said she didn't want to join any club that would **tease** its new members."
Write a sentence using **tease**.

_____

_____

b. **Ridicule** can mean to <u>make fun of</u>. For example, "The counselor explained why it is cruel to **ridicule** another student."
Write a sentence using **ridicule**.

_____

_____

c. **Mock** can mean to <u>make fun of</u>. For example, "My brother and I **mock** each other all the time."
Write a sentence using **mock**.

_____

_____

Word Meaning in Context

Quiz began in the Latin language as a word meaning "who are you?"
Later, in the English language, this meaning expanded to include four
current meanings:

- ❑ **question repeatedly**
- ❑ **practical joke**
- ❑ **short written test**
- ❑ **make fun of**

1. My brother says his friends always **quiz** him because he's the smallest boy in the class.

Which of the meanings of **quiz** is this?_____

_____

2. The police wanted to **quiz** every bystander to determine if anyone could give a good
description of the robber.

Which of the meanings of **quiz** is this?_____

_____

3. On April 1st, many people try to play a **quiz** on their friends.

Which of the meanings of **quiz** is this?_____

_____

4. My math teacher likes to give a pop **quiz** every week to make sure the class understands what
is being covered in class.

Which of the meanings of **quiz** is this?_____

_____

Word Meaning Map   The teacher will give you the **Quiz** worksheet.

Complete Each Definition

1. **Quiz** can mean to interrogate or _____
repeatedly.

2. **Quiz** can also mean a hoax or practical _____.

3. **Quiz** can also mean an exam or short written _____.

4. **Quiz** can also mean to mock or make _____ of someone.

✔ Understanding Check

Circle whether **quiz** is used as you would expect.

1. My parents were very upset when I came home late from school two days in a row. They began to **quiz** me about everything I was doing after school.

   Expect   Not Expect

2. At the end of each school year, the students take an all-day exam that covers everything they studied during the year. They usually start studying for this **quiz** two weeks prior to taking it.

   Expect   Not Expect

3. The Harlem Globetrotters are famous for combining basketball with comedy. They always try to do a **quiz** on one of the referees or a fan in the audience to make everyone laugh.

   Expect   Not Expect

4. My sister tried to tint her hair but messed up and dyed it bright orange instead. I couldn't stop laughing and would **quiz** her every time I saw her.

   Expect   Not Expect

5. I've noticed that my best friend rarely speaks with her parents, and they never ask her about where she goes or what she does after school. When she gets home, they just sit quietly and **quiz** each other.

   Expect   Not Expect

6. Mrs. Smith told everyone to clear their desks and take out a pencil and sheet of paper. Everyone in the class knew we were about to take a pop **quiz**.

   Expect   Not Expect

7. I went with my family last night to see a very sad movie. My mother said it was a tearjerker because everyone in the movie was sad and would always **quiz** each other.

   Expect   Not Expect

8. Johnny needed to go to the principal's office for clowning around in class. He thought the principal wouldn't call his mom if he promised to apologize to the teacher and pull a **quiz** on her once he was sent back to class.

   Expect   Not Expect

Create Stories

On a sheet of paper, write a short story or scenario for each of the four meanings of **quiz**.

Pre-Lesson Activity—Meanings of Related Words

1 One meaning of **ragged** includes the following related words.

   a. **Messy** can mean <u>uncared for</u>. For example, "When I wake up in the morning my hair looks extremely **messy**."

   Write a sentence using **messy**.

   _____

   _____

   b. **Neglected** can mean <u>uncared for</u>. For example, "The stray puppy was skinny and looked **neglected**."

   Write a sentence using **neglected**.

   _____

   _____

   c. **Scruffy** can mean <u>uncared for</u>. For example, "The homeless man had been wearing the same clothes every day and looked **scruffy**."

   Write a sentence using **scruffy**.

   _____

   _____

2 A second meaning of **ragged** includes the following related words.

   a. **Tattered** can mean <u>torn or worn out</u>. For example, "My dad's favorite coat is an old, **tattered** leather jacket he's owned for years."

   Write a sentence using **tattered**.

   _____

   _____

b. **Holey** can mean <u>torn or worn out</u>. For example, "My sister refuses to throw out her favorite pair of jeans even though they're getting **holey**."

Write a sentence using **holey**.

_____

_____

c. **Frayed** can mean <u>torn or worn out</u>. For example, "My mother has an old **frayed** quilt that was made by my great-grandmother."

Write a sentence using **frayed**.

_____

_____

3 A third meaning of **ragged** includes the following related words.

a. **Jagged** can mean <u>imperfect or uneven</u>. For example, "My brother cut his foot when he stepped on a broken bottle with a **jagged** edge."

Write a sentence using **jagged**.

_____

_____

b. **Rough** can mean <u>imperfect or uneven</u>. For example, "The back country road was **rough** and filled with pot holes."

Write a sentence using **rough**.

_____

_____

c. **Notched** can mean <u>imperfect or uneven</u>. For example, "The garden was lined with old railroad ties that were worn and **notched**."

Write a sentence using **notched**.

_____

_____

Word Meaning in Context

Ragged began in the Middle English language as a word meaning "rough or shaggy." Later, the meanings expanded to include three current meanings:

- ❏ **uncared for**
- ❏ **torn or worn out**
- ❏ **imperfect or uneven**

1. The **ragged** cliffs of the mountain made them difficult to climb.

Which of the meanings of **ragged** is this?_____

_____

2. The wild mustang's coat was **ragged** and covered with dirt.

Which of the meanings of **ragged** is this?_____

_____

3. My mother threw out my dog's favorite chew toy because it was too **ragged**.

Which of the meanings of **ragged** is this?_____

_____

Word Meaning Map   The teacher will give you the **Ragged** worksheet.

Complete Each Definition

1. **Ragged** can mean messy or _____ for.

2. **Ragged** can also mean rough, imperfect, or _____.

3. **Ragged** can also mean tattered, _____, or worn out.

Understanding Check

Circle whether **ragged** is used as you would expect.

1. Most pool decks are made of a nonskid material to prevent people from slipping. This **ragged** material helps people keep traction while walking on a wet surface.   Expect   Not Expect

2. The Washington Monument is located within a highly manicured national park in our nation's capital. The area looks **ragged** because it is neatly mowed and litter is picked up quickly.   Expect   Not Expect

3. The house at the end of the street has been abandoned for several years. The house looks **ragged** because the paint is peeling off and the windows are broken.   Expect   Not Expect

4. It is very important for race cars to be as smooth and aerodynamic as possible to reduce drag. Engineers that build these cars make sure every edge is **ragged** so they can reach faster speeds.   Expect   Not Expect

5. When an American flag starts to become **ragged**, it shouldn't be thrown out. It is recommended that the flag be burned to prevent the possibility of it ever being disgraced.   Expect   Not Expect

6. My sister just bought a new dress for her prom. Everyone said she looked great in the **ragged** dress.   Expect   Not Expect

Create Stories

On a sheet of paper, write a short story or scenario for each of the three meanings of **ragged**.

**Ray**

Pre-Lesson Activity—Meanings of Related Words

1 One meaning of **ray** includes the following related words.

a. **Beam** can mean a <u>small amount of light or hopefulness</u>. For example, "A **beam** of sunlight broke through the clouds."

Write a sentence using **beam**.

_____

_____

b. **Glimmer** can mean a <u>small amount of light or hopefulness</u>. For example, "A person who is an optimist always has a **glimmer** of hope regardless of the challenge."

Write a sentence using **glimmer**.

_____

_____

c. **Flicker** can mean a <u>small amount of light or hopefulness</u>. For example, "The campfire gave off a **flicker** before it ignited."

Write a sentence using **flicker**.

_____

_____

2 A second meaning of **ray** includes the following related word.

a. **Stingray** can mean a <u>marine animal with a flattened body and whip-like tail</u>. For example, "The **stingray** is a bottom dweller that lies like a rug on the seafloor."

Write a sentence using **stingray**.

_____

_____

3 A third meaning of **ray** has no related words.

   a. When **ray** is used in this way, it means a <u>line extending from a point</u>. For example, "In math class we learned that if one **ray** is parallel to another, the lines will never intersect."

   Write a sentence using **ray**.

   _____

   _____

Word Meaning in Context

Ray began in the Latin language as a word meaning "be significant in." Later, in the English language, this meaning changed and expanded to include three current meanings:

- ❑ **small amount of light or hopefulness**
- ❑ **marine animal with a flattened body and whip-like tail**
- ❑ **line extending from a point**

1. In math class, we practiced drawing a **ray**.

   Which of the meanings of **ray** is this?_____

   _____

2. I didn't think I had a **ray** of hope for winning the lottery.

   Which of the meanings of **ray** is this?_____

   _____

3. The **ray** is related to the shark family but is not dangerous to humans.

   Which of the meanings of **ray** is this?_____

   _____

Word Meaning Map

The teacher will give you the **Ray** worksheet.

Complete Each Definition

1. **Ray** can mean a glint or a _____ amount of light or hopefulness.

2. **Ray** can also mean a marine animal with a _____ body and whip-like tail.

3. **Ray** can also mean a math term describing a _____ extending from a point.

Understanding Check

Circle whether **ray** is used as you would expect.

1. The Cayman Islands have become a famous place where people can swim close to a **ray**. Many scuba divers and snorkelers visit the island to get the chance to swim and feed these animals.   Expect   Not Expect

2. The art teacher had us practice drawing circles to make smiley faces. It took a lot of practice to draw the perfect **ray** freehand.   Expect   Not Expect

3. The principal used a laser pointer when she spoke in front of the school inside the auditorium. The laser gave off a small **ray** of light that she used to point to her presentation.   Expect   Not Expect

4. The scuba diver saw a great white shark near the shipwreck. He decided not to swim near the wreck because the **ray** was nearby.   Expect   Not Expect

5. In geography class we drew a **ray** across the map of the United States. We wanted to see how many states you would have to go through traveling from coast to coast.   Expect   Not Expect

6. The weatherman said the chance of the blizzard hitting us was 100 %. When I heard this, I knew there might be a **ray** of hope that we would not get any snow.   Expect   Not Expect

Create Stories

On a sheet of paper, write a short story or scenario for each of the three meanings of **ray**.

Reflection

 ## Pre-Lesson Activity—Meanings of Related Words

1 One meaning of **reflection** includes the following related words.

a. **Mirror image** can mean a <u>return of light, heat, or sound after striking a surface</u>. For example, "Smooth and shiny objects can produce a **mirror image** because they return light onto other surfaces."

Write a sentence using **mirror image**.

_____

_____

b. **Echo** can mean a <u>return of light, heat, or sound after striking a surface</u>. For example, "Dolphins can locate fish and other objects underwater by making a clicking sound and then listening for the **echo** it creates once it hits an object."

Write a sentence using **echo**.

_____

_____

c. **Return** can mean a <u>return of light, heat, or sound after striking a surface</u>. For example, "Air traffic controllers look at an airplane's radar **return** to help them land airplanes safely at night and in poor weather conditions."

Write a sentence using **return**.

_____

_____

2 A second meaning of **reflection** includes the following related words.

a. **Thinking** can mean <u>thoughts on something</u>. For example, "Before every move in a chess game, most players seem to be doing deep **thinking**."

Write a sentence using **thinking**.

_____

_____

b. **Meditation** can mean <u>thoughts on something</u>. For example, "The karate instructor told his students that **meditation** was an important aspect of the martial arts."

Write a sentence using **meditation**.

_____

_____

c. **Contemplation** can mean <u>thoughts on something</u>. For example, "My mother warns that if people don't take time out of their day for **contemplation**, they can become very stressed."

Write a sentence using **contemplation**.

_____

_____

3 A third meaning of **reflection** includes the following related words.

a. **Result** can mean an <u>indication of something</u>. For example, "Diane's achievements are a **result** of her hard work."

Write a sentence using **result**.

_____

_____

b. **Sign** can mean an <u>indication of something</u>. For example, "The football coach thought the boy's increased size was a **sign** that he spent a lot of time lifting weights over the summer."

Write a sentence using **sign**.

_____

_____

c. **Evidence** can mean an <u>indication of something</u>. For example, "Tom's failing grade in math was **evidence** that he was not studying."

Write a sentence using **evidence**.

_____

_____

Word Meaning in Context

Reflection began in the Latin language as a word meaning "back or to bend." Later, in the English language, the meanings changed and expanded to include three current meanings:

- ❏ **return of light, heat, or sound after striking a surface**
- ❏ **thoughts on something**
- ❏ **indication of something**

1. The school's high graduation rate was a **reflection** of all the teachers' efforts.

Which of the meanings of **reflection** is this? _____

_____

2. The young boy saw his **reflection** in the pond while he was fishing.

Which of the meanings of **reflection** is this? _____

_____

3. At my great-grandma's funeral, the pastor asked everyone to take a moment for **reflection** on how she touched everyone's lives.

Which of the meanings of **reflection** is this? _____

_____

Word Meaning Map   The teacher will give you the **Reflection** worksheet.

Complete Each Definition

1. **Reflection** can mean a mirror image or return of light, heat, or sound

after striking a _____.

2. **Reflection** can also mean meditation or _____ on something.

3. **Reflection** can also mean the result or _____ of something.

✔ Understanding Check

Circle whether **reflection** is used as you would expect.

1. A mirror gives a **reflection** of whatever is in front of it. The reflected image is made up of particles of light called photons.   Expect   Not Expect

2. I have a four-year-old baby brother. When he is awake, he never sits still for a second, so I can tell he spends a lot of time in **reflection**.   Expect   Not Expect

3. The small child was throwing a tantrum in the store. Everyone thought the behavior of the child was a **reflection** of the parents' way of childrearing.   Expect   Not Expect

4. Submarines are covered with a special material that absorbs radar to make it more difficult to detect. This is important because submarines try to have a **reflection** so enemy ships cannot find them.   Expect   Not Expect

5. Debbie was upset after arguing with her best friend. She sat alone in deep **reflection** trying to understand what started the argument.   Expect   Not Expect

6. I never studied for Spanish and took the final exam in Spanish class. I got 100% on the exam. I knew it was a **reflection** of all of my studying.   Expect   Not Expect

Create Stories

On a sheet of paper, write a short story or scenario for each of the three meanings of **reflection**.

Roller

Pre-Lesson Activity—Meanings of Related Words

1 One meaning of **roller** includes the following related words.

a. **Curling iron** can mean <u>something used to curl hair</u>. For example, "My mother warned me to be careful if I used her bathroom because her **curling iron** was plugged in."

Write a sentence using **curling iron**.

_____

_____

b. **Curler** can mean <u>something used to curl hair</u>. For example, "My sister forgot and left one **curler** in her hair when she left for school."

Write a sentence using **curler**.

_____

_____

c. A **perm** is a process or <u>something used to curl hair</u>. For example, "My mother thought that I should get a **perm** if I want to have hair like Carol's."

Write a sentence using **perm**.

_____

_____

2 A second meaning of **roller** includes the following related words.

a. **Swell** can mean a <u>long wave</u>. For example, "A large **swell** hit the canoe and capsized it."

Write a sentence using **swell**.

_____

_____

b. **Breaker** can mean a <u>long wave</u>. For example, "The surfer paddled his board through a large **breaker**."

Write a sentence using **breaker**.

_____

_____

c. **Surf** can mean a <u>long wave</u>. For example, "It's relaxing to sit on the beach and watch the **surf** in the distance."

Write a sentence using **surf**.

_____

_____

3 A third meaning of **roller** includes the following related words.

a. **Rolling pin** can mean a <u>cylinder used for flattening or spreading things</u>. For example, "The best part about making pie crusts is using the **rolling pin** to flatten out the dough."

Write a sentence using **rolling pin**.

_____

_____

b. **Rolling dowel** can mean a <u>cylinder used for flattening or spreading things</u>. For example, "I like visiting the bakery to watch the baker make pastries with the **rolling dowel**."

Write a sentence using **rolling dowel**.

_____

_____

4 A fourth meaning of **roller** has no related words.

a. When **roller** is used in this way, it means a <u>small spokeless wheel</u>. For example, "I fell down and scraped my knee when my skate lost a **roller**."

Write a sentence using **roller**.

_____

_____

Word Meaning in Context

Roller began in the Latin language as a word meaning "small wheel." Later, in the English language, this meaning expanded to include four current meanings:

- ❑ **something used to curl hair**
- ❑ **long wave**
- ❑ **cylinder used for flattening or spreading things**
- ❑ **small spokeless wheel**

1. I can tell when I need a new **roller** for my skateboard because it will begin to make a lot of noise.

Which of the meanings of **roller** is this? _____

_____

2. I bought my sister a cordless **roller** for her birthday.

Which of the meanings of **roller** is this? _____

_____

3. The jet skiers tried to jump the big **roller** to get some airtime.

Which of the meanings of **roller** is this? _____

_____

4. My mother used a **roller** to spread out the cookie dough on the kitchen counter.

Which of the meanings of **roller** is this? _____

_____

Word Meaning Map   The teacher will give you the **Roller** worksheet.

Complete Each Definition

1. **Roller** can mean a curling iron or something used to curl _____.

2. **Roller** can also mean a swell or long _____.

3. **Roller** can also mean a rolling pin or _____ used for flattening or spreading things.

4. **Roller** can also mean a small spokeless _____.

Understanding Check

Circle whether **roller** is used as you would expect.

1. My sister was so embarrassed this morning at school. Her friend pointed out to her that she forgot to take out a **roller** in the back of her hair.

   Expect   Not Expect

2. Brian spent ten minutes changing a flat tire on his mountain bike. He needed to change the tube on the **roller**.

   Expect   Not Expect

3. My grandpa showed me how to make pizza from scratch. He let me spread the pizza dough with a **roller**.

   Expect   Not Expect

4. A lot of surfers like to visit Hawaii's North Shore. They like the chance to surf an incredibly large **roller**.

   Expect   Not Expect

5. While the couch was quite heavy, it was very easy to move. The couch glided across the hardwood floor because we replaced each leg with a **roller**.

   Expect   Not Expect

6. My brother's hair is always a mess when he wakes up. We tell him that he doesn't even look human until he combs his hair with a **roller**.

   Expect   Not Expect

7. James was skipping stones across the pond. After the stone hit the water, it produced a **roller**.

   Expect   Not Expect

8. I was making cookie dough with my sister. We put all of the ingredients into the **roller** and mixed them together.

   Expect   Not Expect

Create Stories

On a sheet of paper, write a short story or scenario for each of the four meanings of **roller**.

Pre-Lesson Activity—Meanings of Related Words

1 One meaning of **rub** includes the following related words.

a. **Massage** can mean to <u>place pressure using a back-and-forth motion</u>. For example, "A masseuse is a person trained to **massage** people's sore muscles."
Write a sentence using **massage**.

_____

_____

b. **Buff** can mean to <u>place pressure using a back-and-forth motion</u>. For example, "My mother asked me to **buff** the silverware we will be using for the company coming over for dinner tonight."
Write a sentence using **buff**.

_____

_____

c. **Caress** can mean to <u>place pressure using a back-and-forth motion</u>. For example, "My cat loves it when you **caress** her behind the ears."
Write a sentence using **caress**.

_____

_____

2 A second meaning of **rub** includes the following related words.

a. **Apply** can mean to <u>cover with</u>. For example, "During the cold winter months, my mother makes sure to **apply** hand lotion every day to prevent her hands from cracking."
Write a sentence using **apply**.

_____

_____

b. **Put on** can mean to <u>cover with</u>. For example, "Before I go to the beach, I make sure I **put on** sunscreen all over my face and neck."
Write a sentence using **put on**.

_____

_____

c. **Smear** can mean to <u>cover with</u>. For example, "The recipe said to **smear** orange sauce all over the duck before baking it." Write a sentence using **smear**.

_____

_____

3 A third meaning of **rub** includes the following related words.

a. **Trouble** can mean <u>something that annoys</u>. For example, "The **trouble** with being sick is that I have to play catch up in all of my classes the first day back at school." Write a sentence using **trouble**.

_____

_____

b. **Difficulty** can mean <u>something that annoys</u>. For example, "The **difficulty** with having an older brother is that you're always being compared to him." Write a sentence using **difficulty**.

_____

_____

c. **Pitfall** can mean <u>something that annoys</u>. For example, "For me, the **pitfall** of getting detention is that I miss the school bus and have to walk home from school." Write a sentence using **pitfall**.

_____

_____

4 A fourth meaning of **rub** includes the following related words.

a. **Clear** can mean to <u>remove by wiping</u>. For example, "We asked the waitress to **clear** the table before we sat down." Write a sentence using **clear**.

_____

_____

b. **Expunge** can mean to <u>remove by wiping</u>. For example, "The spot remover claimed it could **expunge** almost any stain." Write a sentence using **expunge**.

_____

_____

c. **Erase** can mean to <u>remove by wiping</u>. For example, "James realized he forgot an important step in his math homework, so he had to **erase** his answer and do it again." Write a sentence using **erase**.

_____

_____

Word Meaning in Context

Rub began in the German language as a word meaning "scratch." Later, in the English language, this meaning changed and expanded to include four current meanings:

- ❑ **place pressure using a back-and-forth motion**
- ❑ **cover with**
- ❑ **something that annoys**
- ❑ **remove by wiping**

1. The student changed his answer on the test and had to **rub** out his first answer.

Which of the meanings of **rub** is this? _____

_____

2. My mother has to **rub** my baby brother's back to help him fall asleep at night.

Which of the meanings of **rub** is this? _____

_____

3. The cookbook said to **rub** the cookie pan with margarine to prevent the cookies from sticking.

Which of the meanings of **rub** is this? _____

_____

4. The **rub** with getting a speeding ticket is that my insurance rates are going to increase.

Which of the meanings of **rub** is this? _____

_____

Word Meaning Map   The teacher will give you the **Rub** worksheet.

Complete Each Definition

1. **Rub** can mean to caress or place pressure using a back-and-forth

_____.

2. **Rub** can also mean to apply or _____ with.

3. **Rub** can also mean trouble or something that _____.

4. **Rub** can also mean to erase or _____ by wiping.

Understanding Check

Circle whether **rub** is used as you would expect.

1. Skin cancer is the most common cancer in the United States. Doctors recommend that everyone should **rub** sunscreen on if they spend a lot of time outdoors.

    Expect   Not Expect

2. Julie is my best friend and we enjoy hanging out together. Therefore, it seems to **rub** me whenever I see her.

    Expect   Not Expect

3. My father hurt his back shoveling snow from the driveway. Now, every time I see him, he asks if I can **rub** his back.

    Expect   Not Expect

4. The school nurse gently dabbed antibacterial cream onto my scraped knee with a cotton swab. She made sure to **rub** the medicine on because she knew the scrape stung.

    Expect   Not Expect

5. Tammy spilt ketchup all over her pants. She ran to the bathroom to try and **rub** out the stain.

    Expect   Not Expect

6. The doctor said he was going to freeze the wart off the patient's hand with just a drop of liquid nitrogen. The doctor made sure to **rub** the patient's hand with liquid nitrogen.

    Expect   Not Expect

7. Cindy is always arguing with the new girl in school. Cindy says the girl always seems to **rub** her the wrong way.

    Expect   Not Expect

8. The secretaries use white correction fluid to cover up any of their typing mistakes. It will **rub** out any mistake once it dries.

    Expect   Not Expect

Create Stories

On a sheet of paper, write a short story or scenario for each of the four meanings of **rub**.

|  # Scene

Pre-Lesson Activity—Meanings of Related Words

1 One meaning of **scene** includes the following related words.

a. **Site** can mean a <u>location where something takes or has taken place</u>. For example, "The Little Big Horn National Monument is in the state of Montana at the **site** of General Custer's last stand."
Write a sentence using **site**.

_____

_____

b. **Spot** can mean a <u>location where something takes or has taken place</u>. For example, "The police were investigating the **spot** where the crime happened."
Write a sentence using **spot**.

_____

_____

c. **Locale** can mean a <u>location where something takes or has taken place</u>. For example, "The Lewis and Clark Trail allows hikers to see the same **locale** the explorers viewed along the Missouri and Columbia rivers."
Write a sentence using **locale**.

_____

_____

2 A second meaning of **scene** includes the following related words.

a. **Landscape** can mean a <u>view</u>. For example, "From the top of the Grand Canyon, visitors can see a beautiful **landscape** carved over time by the Colorado River."
Write a sentence using **landscape**.

_____

_____

b. **Scenery** can mean a <u>view</u>. For example, "My parents like to go hiking in the mountains and take pictures of the beautiful **scenery**."
Write a sentence using **scenery**.

_____

_____

c. **Vista** can mean a <u>view</u>. For example, "The hikers stopped to enjoy the **vista** when they reached the top of the mountain." Write a sentence using **vista**.

_____

_____

3 A third meaning of **scene** includes the following related words.

a. **Tantrum** can mean an <u>embarrassing display of anger or bad manners</u>. For example, "The little boy had a **tantrum** in the store when his mother refused to buy him a toy." Write a sentence using **tantrum**.

_____

_____

b. **Outburst** can mean an <u>embarrassing display of anger or bad manners</u>. For example, "My little sister's **outburst** at the state fair only lasted for a few minutes, but it was still very embarassing." Write a sentence using **outburst**.

_____

_____

c. **Fuss** can mean an <u>embarrassing display of anger or bad manners</u>. For example, "The lady at the service desk was very patient when the customer caused a **fuss**." Write a sentence using **fuss**.

_____

_____

4 A fourth meaning of **scene** includes the following related words.

a. **Act** can mean <u>part of a movie or play</u>. For example, "My favorite **act** from the play _Romeo and Juliet_ was when Romeo's best friend Mercutio gets into a sword fight." Write a sentence using **act**.

_____

_____

b. **Sketch** can mean part of a <u>movie or play</u>. For example, "Abbott and Costello's baseball **sketch** about "Who's on First" is hilarious." Write a sentence using **sketch**.

_____

_____

c. **Performance** can mean <u>part of a movie or play</u>. For example, "My mother was watching a **performance** from the Swan Lake ballet on television." Write a sentence using **performance**.

_____

_____

Word Meaning in Context

Scene began in the Latin language as a word meaning "stage." Later, in the English language, this meaning expanded to include four current meanings:

- ❏ **location where something takes or has taken place**
- ❏ **view**
- ❏ **embarrassing display of anger or bad manners**
- ❏ **part of a movie or play**

1. My dad turned off the movie I was watching during my favorite **scene** and told me to do my homework.

Which of the meanings of **scene** is this?_____

_____

2. The thief was caught when he went back to the **scene** of the crime.

Which of the meanings of **scene** is this?_____

_____

3. Tourists like to visit the northeast during the fall to watch the colorful **scene** of leaves changing colors.

Which of the meanings of **scene** is this?_____

_____

4. My Aunt Sally loves to tell everyone the story of how I made a **scene** while she was baby-sitting me when I was two years old.

Which of the meanings of **scene** is this?_____

_____

Word Meaning Map   The teacher will give you the **Scene** worksheet.

Complete Each Definition

1. **Scene** can mean a site or _____
where something takes or has taken place.

2. **Scene** can also mean scenery or a _____.

3. **Scene** can also mean an act or _____ of a movie or play.

4. **Scene** can also mean a tantrum or _____
display of anger or bad manners.

Understanding Check

Circle whether **scene** is used as you would expect.

1. My friend Tim called 911 immediately after he saw the car accident. The operator said an ambulance would be on the **scene** within minutes.   Expect   Not Expect

2. My dad started yelling at the waiter because his food was cold. My mother told him not to make a **scene** in the restaurant.   Expect   Not Expect

3. I was touring Hollywood studios when I saw Beyoncé. I asked for her autograph because she is my favorite **scene**.   Expect   Not Expect

4. Janice said she would meet me at the movies at 9 o'clock. She showed up a half hour later than the agreed upon **scene**.   Expect   Not Expect

5. My Aunt Joan is the sweetest person and never seems to get upset at anyone. Her favorite saying is to make a **scene** by letting insults roll off your back like water on a duck.   Expect   Not Expect

6. My brother and I have the *Finding Nemo* video at home. We each try to memorize our favorite **scene** from the movie.   Expect   Not Expect

7. My mother loves to sunbathe at the beach. She says it is very relaxing to just sit back and enjoy the **scene**.   Expect   Not Expect

8. The lights in our house went out last night during the electrical storm. It was pitch black in the house, and all I could see was the **scene**.   Expect   Not Expect

Create Stories

On a sheet of paper, write a short story or scenario for each of the four meanings of **scene**.

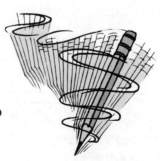

The Multiple Meaning Vocabulary Program

Scramble

Pre-Lesson Activity—Meanings of Related Words

1 One meaning of **scramble** includes the following related words.

a. **Hurry** can mean to <u>move without delay</u>. For example, "I told my friend to **hurry** or we would be late for the movies."

Write a sentence using **hurry**.

_____

_____

b. **Rush** can mean to <u>move without delay</u>. For example, "In P. E. class, we were supposed to **rush** through the obstacle course as quickly as we could."

Write a sentence using **rush**.

_____

_____

c. **Scurry** can mean to <u>move without delay</u>. For example, "The neighbor's cat would always **scurry** through the backyard in case our dog was outside."

Write a sentence using **scurry**.

_____

_____

2 A second meaning of **scramble** includes the following related words.

a. **Mix up** can mean to <u>mix together</u>. For example, "My mother always asks me to **mix up** the ingredients when she cooks."

Write a sentence using **mix up**.

_____

_____

b. **Combine** can mean to <u>mix together</u>. For example, "My dad let me **combine** all of the ingredients into a bowl when we made the omelet."

Write a sentence using **combine**.

_____

_____

c. **Blend** can mean to <u>mix together</u>. For example, "The nice thing about a breadmaker is that it will automatically **blend** all of the ingredients you put into it."

Write a sentence using **blend**.

_____

_____

3 A third meaning of **scramble** includes the following related word.

a. **Encode** can mean <u>make a radio or TV signal mixed up</u>. For example, "The military will **encode** all of its communications during war time to prevent enemies from understanding what is being said."

Write a sentence using **encode**.

_____

_____

Word Meaning in Context

Scramble began in the Dutch language as a word meaning "leave rapidly." Later, in the English language, this meaning expanded to include three current meanings:

- ❑ **move without delay**
- ❑ **mix together**
- ❑ **make a radio or TV signal mixed up**

1. The fighter pilots had to **scramble** to their jets for an alert launch.

Which of the meanings of **scramble** is this? _____

_____

2. I like to **scramble** my eggs with ham, onions, and green peppers.

Which of the meanings of **scramble** is this? _____

_____

3. The cable company will **scramble** its signal to prevent people from watching their shows without paying a fee.

Which of the meanings of **scramble** is this? _____

_____

Word Meaning Map   The teacher will give you the **Scramble** worksheet.

Complete Each Definition

1. **Scramble** can mean to hurry or _____ without delay.

2. **Scramble** can also mean to combine or _____ together.

3. **Scramble** can also mean to encode or make a radio or TV _____ or unintelligible.

Understanding Check

Circle whether **scramble** is used as you would expect.

1. I just heard on the radio that my favorite band is coming to town. I think I'll have to **scramble** to get tickets before they're sold out.

   Expect   Not Expect

2. The recipe called for six different ingredients. It said to chop them up and **scramble** them together before baking.

   Expect   Not Expect

3. My dad ordered a movie channel so we wouldn't have to go to the video store all the time. The cable company had to install a special box so we could **scramble** the signal to watch the movies.

   Expect   Not Expect

4. Jim likes eating in the cafeteria where they serve every side of food on a separate plate. He likes it when they **scramble** the food together like that.

   Expect   Not Expect

5. I like listening to the hip-hop radio stations on the stereo. My parents don't like the music, however, and always tell me to **scramble** the station when they come home.

   Expect   Not Expect

6. My great-grandfather is nearly a hundred years old and moves very slowly. When he walks around the house, it takes him a while to **scramble** from room to room.

   Expect   Not Expect

Create Stories

On a sheet of paper, write a short story or scenario for each of the three meanings of **scramble**.

Settle

Pre-Lesson Activity—Meanings of Related Words

1 One meaning of **settle** includes the following related words.

a. **Colonize** can mean to <u>live or be established in a desired position</u>. For example, "During the 16th century, Spain was one of the few European countries that was successful in trying to **colonize** the Americas."
Write a sentence using **colonize**.

_____

_____

b. **Take up residence** can mean to <u>live or be established in a desired position</u>. For example, "My brother decided to **take up residence** in Colorado because he liked skiing in the Rocky Mountains."
Write a sentence using **take up residence**.

_____

_____

c. **Put down roots** can mean to <u>live or be established in a desired position</u>. For example, "My grandparents came from Ireland to **put down roots** in the United States."
Write a sentence using **put down roots**.

_____

_____

2 A second meaning of **settle** includes the following related words.

a. **Resolve** can mean to <u>clear up a dispute</u>. For example, "The driver stopped the school bus and said he wouldn't continue until the two boys who were arguing decided to **resolve** their differences."
Write a sentence using **resolve**.

_____

_____

b. **Straighten out** can mean to <u>clear up a dispute</u>. For example, "Jenny called her best friend after they argued to **straighten out** any hard feelings."
Write a sentence using **straighten out**.

_____

_____

c. **Agree** can mean to <u>clear up a dispute</u>. For example, "After an hour of bickering, the

two brothers finally decided to **agree** on what movie they would rent."
Write a sentence using **agree**.

_____

_____

3 A third meaning of **settle** includes the following related words.

a. **Quiet** can mean to <u>restore calm or to return something to its natural state</u>. For example, "The last time we had a substitute teacher, the principal had to come into our room and ask everyone to **quiet** down."
Write a sentence using **quiet**.

_____

_____

b. **Relax** can mean to <u>restore calm or to return something to its natural state</u>. For example, "My mother practices yoga to try and **relax** herself at the end of a busy day."
Write a sentence using **relax**.

_____

_____

c. **Calm** can mean to <u>restore calm or to return something to its natural state</u>. For example, "It took the class all morning to **calm** down after we found out we would be going to the amusement park for our field trip."
Write a sentence using **calm**.

_____

_____

4 A fourth meaning of **settle** includes the following related words.

a. **Go lower** means to <u>sink</u>. For example, "The heavier it rained, the more the car's tires would **go lower** into the muddy dirt road." Write a sentence using **go lower**.

_____

_____

b. **Descend** can mean to <u>sink</u>. For example, "I think the rear tire is flat because the back of the car seems to **descend**." Write a sentence using **descend**.

_____

_____

c. **Slump** can mean to <u>sink</u>. For example, "The TV news showed a picture of a house that began to **slump** into some swamp land."
Write a sentence using **slump**.

_____

_____

Word Meaning in Context

Settle began in the Old English language as a word meaning "a seat." Later, this meaning changed and expanded to include four current meanings:

- ❑ **live or be established in a desired position**
- ❑ **clear up a dispute**
- ❑ **restore calm or return something to its natural state**
- ❑ **sink**

1. The heavy bulldozer began to **settle** into the grass field when the ground was soggy last spring.

Which of the meanings of **settle** is this? _____

_____

2. While people from the Amish community live in 22 states, the largest number decided to **settle** in Lancaster County, Pennsylvania.

Which of the meanings of **settle** is this? _____

_____

3. The teacher asked the students to try and **settle** their argument.

Which of the meanings of **settle** is this? _____

_____

4. The waves began to **settle** down after the storm passed through.

Which of the meanings of **settle** is this? _____

_____

Word Meaning Map   The teacher will give you the **Settle** worksheet.

Complete Each Definition

1. **Settle** can mean to take up residence or be _____ in a desired position.

2. **Settle** can also mean to relax, calm, or _____ something to its natural state.

3. **Settle** can also mean to go lower or _____.

4. **Settle** can also mean to agree or _____ up a dispute.

Understanding Check

Circle whether **settle** is used as you would expect.

1. My sister wants to be a doctor when she grows up. She said she would not **settle** for anything else.

   Expect   Not Expect

2. After the referee made a bad call, the fans began to yell. It took several minutes for the crowd to **settle** down.

   Expect   Not Expect

3. My Uncle Harry is very funny, but he is always picking on somebody. Whenever he comes into a room, you can be sure he will **settle** things down.

   Expect   Not Expect

4. I tried to walk across a field that was covered with several feet of snow. I could not walk very far because my feet would **settle** into the deep snow.

   Expect   Not Expect

5. My dad is going to visit New York for the weekend. He will **settle** there only for a few days.

   Expect   Not Expect

6. My two sisters are always fighting. I wish they could **settle** their arguing once and for all.

   Expect   Not Expect

7. I was helping my mom bake bread last night. I added yeast to the dough to help it **settle**.

   Expect   Not Expect

8. Jess was playing with my mom's snow globes at Christmas time. To create a blizzard, you have to **settle** the globe violently then set it down and watch it snow.

   Expect   Not Expect

Create Stories

On a sheet of paper, write a short story or scenario for each of the four meanings of **settle**.

Shower

Pre-Lesson Activity—Meanings of Related Words

1 One meaning of **shower** includes the following related words.

   a. **Drizzle** can mean a <u>brief fall of rain or snow</u>. For example, "Although it was only supposed to **drizzle**, I thought I would bring an umbrella."

   Write a sentence using **drizzle**.

   _____

   _____

   b. **Flurry** can mean a <u>brief fall of rain or snow</u>. For example, "The weather station said we should expect a snow **flurry** tonight."

   Write a sentence using **flurry**.

   _____

   _____

   c. **Downfall** can mean a <u>brief fall of rain or snow</u>. For example, "The baseball game was temporarily delayed due to a sudden **downfall**."

   Write a sentence using **downfall**.

   _____

   _____

2 A second meaning of **shower** includes the following related words.

   a. **Banquet** can mean a <u>party given to honor someone</u>. For example, "We had a **banquet** to celebrate my grandparents' thirty-fifth anniversary."

   Write a sentence using **banquet**.

   _____

   _____

b. **Feast** can mean a <u>party given to honor someone</u>. For example, "The church held a **feast** to celebrate the Christmas season."

Write a sentence using **feast**.

_____

_____

c. **Bash** can mean a <u>party given to honor someone</u>. For example, "My parents held a **bash** for my brother when he graduated from high school."

Write a sentence using **bash**.

_____

_____

3 A third meaning of **shower** includes the following related words.

a. **Lavish** can mean <u>a lot of something</u>. For example, "After Renée hit the game-winning run, her teammates started to **lavish** her with praise."

Write a sentence using **lavish**.

_____

_____

b. **Barrage** can mean <u>a lot of something</u>. For example, "The archers launched a **barrage** of arrows at the enemy."

Write a sentence using **barrage**.

_____

_____

c. **Hail** can mean <u>a lot of something</u>. For example, "The riot police used shields to protect themselves from a **hail** of rocks thrown by the angry mob."

Write a sentence using **hail**.

_____

_____

4 A fourth meaning of **shower** has no related words.

a. When **shower** is used in this way, it means a <u>device in a bathroom used to bathe</u>. For example, "After Kristen was sprayed by a skunk, she spent an hour scrubbing herself in the **shower**."

Write a sentence using **shower**.

_____

_____

Word Meaning in Context

Shower began in the Old English language as a word meaning "a storm or wind." Later, this meaning expanded to include four current meanings:

- ❑ **brief fall of rain or snow**
- ❑ **party given to honor someone**
- ❑ **a lot of something**
- ❑ **device in a bathroom used to bathe**

1. My brother takes such a long **shower**, there is usually no hot water left when he is done.

   Which of the meanings of **shower** is this? _____

   _____

2. Our car seats were soaked because we left the windows down during the rain **shower**.

   Which of the meanings of **shower** is this? _____

   _____

3. The bride received wonderful presents at her wedding **shower**.

   Which of the meanings of **shower** is this? _____

   _____

4. After I got straight A's in school, my parents started to **shower** me with statements about how great I did in school.

   Which of the meanings of **shower** is this? _____

   _____

Word Meaning Map   The teacher will give you the **Shower** worksheet.

Complete Each Definition

1. **Shower** can mean a drizzle or brief _____ of rain or snow.

2. **Shower** can also mean a banquet or party given to _____ someone.

3. **Shower** can also mean a load or a _____ of something.

4. **Shower** can also mean a device in a bathroom used to _____.

✔ Understanding Check

Circle whether **shower** is used as you would expect.

1. My sister will be getting married next month. Next weekend we're going to have a **shower** for her.   Expect   Not Expect

2. When I woke up this morning, the ground outside was wet. There must have been a **shower** in the middle of the night.   Expect   Not Expect

3. My older sister can spend hours in the bathroom getting dressed. She spends at least an hour in front of the **shower** putting on her make up.   Expect   Not Expect

4. Every Valentine's Day, I received at least a dozen cards from my friends. We all try to **shower** each other with affection.   Expect   Not Expect

5. My math teacher has never called on me in class and I doubt he even knows my name. I'm not very happy with how he tries to **shower** me with attention in his class.   Expect   Not Expect

6. It's been raining for three days straight due to the hurricane. The weatherman said this **shower** should stop within the next day or two.   Expect   Not Expect

7. My mother didn't want to celebrate her birthday this year. She decided not to have anyone over but asked for a quiet **shower** instead.   Expect   Not Expect

8. After backpacking for several days, I began to smell like a campfire. Once I got home, I jumped into the **shower** to clean up.   Expect   Not Expect

Create Stories

On a sheet of paper, write a short story or scenario for each of the four meanings of **shower**.

Pre-Lesson Activity—Meanings of Related Words

1 One meaning of **spare** includes the following related words.

a. **Free** can mean to <u>not hurt or harm</u>. For example, "During the Spanish Inquisition, people who were falsely charged with crimes hoped the church would **free** them."

Write a sentence using **free**.

_____

_____

b. **Go easy on** can mean to <u>not hurt or harm</u>. For example, "The students were hoping the math teacher would **go easy on** them with homework tonight."

Write a sentence using **go easy on**.

_____

_____

c. **Show mercy to** can mean to <u>not hurt or harm</u>. For example, "The Geneva Convention tried to ensure that armies would **show mercy to** captured enemy soldiers."

Write a sentence using **show mercy to**.

_____

_____

2 A second meaning of **spare** includes the following related words.

a. **Reserve** can mean an <u>additional item set aside</u>. For example, "A lot of four-wheel-drive vehicles have a **reserve** gas tank, to make sure they don't run out of gas."

Write a sentence using **reserve**.

_____

_____

b. **Extra** can mean an <u>additional item set aside</u>. For example, "When I go hiking, I usually bring an **extra** pair of socks."

Write a sentence using **extra**.

_____

_____

c. **Surplus** can mean an <u>additional item set aside</u>. For example, "If you go camping, you should always bring **surplus** food in case of an emergency."
Write a sentence using **surplus**.

_____

_____

3 A third meaning of **spare** includes the following related words.

a. **Offer** can mean <u>give away</u>. For example, "The small child was begging on the street corner, hoping people would **offer** him some food or money."
Write a sentence using **offer**.

_____

_____

b. **Contribute** can mean <u>give away</u>. For example, "Jerry Lewis hosts a telethon every year that asks people to **contribute** money for children with muscular distrophy."
Write a sentence using **contribute**.

_____

_____

c. **Donate** can mean <u>give away</u>. For example, "The Salvation Army has people who stand outside of department stores during the holiday season to ask shoppers to **donate** money for the poor."
Write a sentence using **donate**.

_____

_____

4 A fourth meaning of **spare** includes the following related words.

a. **Skin and bones** means <u>thin or small</u>. For example, "The survivors of the shipwreck were **skin and bones** by the time they were rescued."
Write a sentence using **skin and bones**.

_____

_____

b. **Meager** can mean <u>thin or small</u>. For example, "The homeless man ate **meager** meals."
Write a sentence using **meager**.

_____

_____

c. **Slender** can mean <u>thin or small</u>. For example, "The distance runners on the track team seemed **slender** when standing next to the sprinters."
Write a sentence using **slender**.

_____

_____

Word Meaning in Context

Spare began in the Old English language as a word meaning "to leap."
Later, this meaning changed and expanded to include four current
meanings:

- ❑ **not hurt or harm**
- ❑ **additional item set aside**
- ❑ **give away**
- ❑ **thin or small**

1. The fashion models were beautiful, but they looked very **spare**, as if they had not
been eating.

Which of the meanings of **spare** is this?_____

_____

2. The general told his men to **spare** any enemy soldier that tried to surrender.

Which of the meanings of **spare** is this?_____

_____

3. I always carry a **spare** bike tube with me when I go riding.

Which of the meanings of **spare** is this?_____

_____

4. The Red Cross asked everyone to see what items or money they could **spare** for the
flood victims.

Which of the meanings of **spare** is this?_____

_____

Word Meaning Map   The teacher will give you the **Spare** worksheet.

Complete Each Definition

1. Spare can mean to show mercy or not _____ or harm.

2. Spare can also mean a reserve, or _____
item set aside.

3. Spare can also mean slender, _____, or small.

4. Spare can also mean to donate or give _____.

Understanding Check

Circle whether **spare** is used as you would expect.

1. Pocahontas was the daughter of a powerful chief of the Algonquian Indians. It is believed she asked her father to **spare** the life of Captain John Smith and helped establish peace between the European settlers and the Indians in Virginia.　　　　Expect　　　Not Expect

2. My dad had a flat tire on his car. It took us a half hour to change it out and put the **spare** tire on.　　　　Expect　　　Not Expect

3. My Uncle Bob is extremely heavy. He is very **spare** since he weighs over 300 pounds.　　　　Expect　　　Not Expect

4. My uncle always tells me how important money is and that I should save everything I can. He says I should never give away my money but **spare** it in the bank.　　　　Expect　　　Not Expect

5. I was served a small meal on the airplane flight. It was very **spare**, with tiny portions of food.　　　　Expect　　　Not Expect

6. My brother and I were downtown when we walked by a homeless man. He asked us if we could **spare** some change.　　　　Expect　　　Not Expect

7. The hikers were getting very thirsty since they forgot to bring water with them. They were starting to dehydrate since they had **spare** water canteens.　　　　Expect　　　Not Expect

8. The class bully would pick on all the new students their first day at school. Today, he decided to **spare** the new student Bobby and shoved him out of line during lunch.　　　　Expect　　　Not Expect

Create Stories

On a sheet of paper, write a short story or scenario for each of the four meanings of **spare**.

The Multiple Meaning Vocabulary Program

Spring

 ## Pre-Lesson Activity—Meanings of Related Words

1 One meaning of **spring** includes the following related words.

a. **Jump** can mean to <u>suddenly move or occur</u>. For example, "Everyone on the winning baseball team began to **jump** in the air once the game was over."

Write a sentence using **jump**.

_____

_____

b. **Leap** can mean to <u>suddenly move or occur</u>. For example, "The dolphins would **leap** out of the water and do a flip in front of the audience at Sea World."

Write a sentence using **leap**.

_____

_____

c. **Shoot up** can mean to <u>suddenly move or occur</u>. For example, "Once the warm weather came, the tulips began to **shoot up** from the ground."

Write a sentence using **shoot up**.

_____

_____

2 A second meaning of **spring** includes the following related words.

a. **Brook** can mean a <u>small stream</u>. For example, "Craig learned how to fly fish at the **brook** in the state park."

Write a sentence using **brook**.

_____

_____

b. **Creek** can mean a <u>small stream</u>. For example, "Grandpa is fishing for catfish down at the **creek**."

Write a sentence using **creek**.

_____

_____

3 A third meaning of **spring** includes the following related word.

a. **Vernal season** can mean the <u>season between March 21 and June 21</u>. For example, "The farmer needed to wait for the **vernal season** before he could plant his crops."

Write a sentence using **vernal season**.

_____

_____

4 A fourth meaning of **spring** has no related words.

a. When **spring** is used in this way, it means a <u>coil that regains its normal shape after being compressed</u>. For example, "The **spring** on a screen door makes sure the door will return to the closed position."

Write a sentence using **spring**.

_____

_____

Word Meaning in Context

Spring began in the Old English language as a word meaning "to leap or fly up." Later, the meanings expanded to include four current meanings:

- ❏ **suddenly move or occur**
- ❏ **small stream**
- ❏ **season between March 21 and June 21**
- ❏ **coil that regains its normal shape after being compressed**

1. The **spring** in the couch was broken, so it was very uncomfortable to sit on for any length of time.

Which of the meanings of **spring** is this?_____

_____

2. All of the soldiers would **spring** to attention whenever the General entered the room.

Which of the meanings of **spring** is this?_____

_____

3. The hikers filled their canteens with water from the **spring**.

Which of the meanings of **spring** is this?_____

_____

4. **Spring** in the state of Virginia is often called "the rainy season."

Which of the meanings of **spring** is this?_____

_____

Word Meaning Map   The teacher will give you the **Spring** worksheet.

Complete Each Definition

1. **Spring** can mean to jump or suddenly _____ or occur.

2. **Spring** can also mean a brook or small _____.

3. **Spring** can also mean the vernal season or _____ between March 21 and June 21.

4. **Spring** can also mean a coil that regains its normal or original _____ after being compressed.

✔ Understanding Check

Circle whether **spring** is used as you would expect.

1. The temperature didn't start to warm up until May this year. This **spring** was unusually cold.

   Expect   Not Expect

2. The **spring** at the bottom of the mountain was very cold. Katy soaked her feet in the water until they began to turn a bluish color.

   Expect   Not Expect

3. Ted takes a long time to wake up in the morning. It usually takes him almost a half hour to **spring** out of bed.

   Expect   Not Expect

4. Jerry can't wait for school to let out for the year. He likes to go camping with his family for most of July during **spring** break.

   Expect   Not Expect

5. Kelly was given a jack-in-the-box for her birthday. She screamed the first time she saw the clown **spring** out of the box.

   Expect   Not Expect

6. Kevin went waterskiing with his brother yesterday on the large lake. During the summer, they ski almost every day on this **spring**.

   Expect   Not Expect

7. Jennifer looked at the old mattress that was in the garage. The bed was beginning to rip apart and she could see a metal **spring** inside of it.

   Expect   Not Expect

8. Brent asked his mother if he could get a new pillow. He said his pillow was ripped and the **spring** was starting to come out.

   Expect   Not Expect

Create Stories

On a sheet of paper, write a short story or scenario for each of the four meanings of **spring**.

Stitch

Pre-Lesson Activity—Meanings of Related Words

1 One meaning of **stitch** includes the following related words.

   a. **Sew** can mean to <u>tie together with staples or thread</u>. For example, "My mother helped me **sew** up a rip in my pants this morning."

     Write a sentence using **sew**.

     _____

     _____

   b. **Mend** can mean to <u>tie together with staples or thread</u>. For example, "I need to **mend** two pairs of my jeans that have holes in them."

     Write a sentence using **mend**.

     _____

     _____

   c. **Repair** can mean to <u>tie together with staples or thread</u>. For example, "We needed to **repair** the couch after our kitten decided to sharpen her claws on it."

     Write a sentence using **repair**.

     _____

     _____

2 A second meaning of **stitch** includes the following related words.

   a. **Spasm** can mean a <u>sudden sharp pain in the abdomen</u>. For example, "After running around the track, I felt a **spasm** in my side."

     Write a sentence using **spasm**.

     _____

     _____

b. **Twinge** can mean a <u>sudden sharp pain in the abdomen</u>. For example, "I had a **twinge** in my stomach while running around the playground after lunch."

Write a sentence using **twinge**.

_____

_____

c. **Pang** can mean a <u>sudden sharp pain in the abdomen</u>. For example, "After playing tennis for over an hour, I felt a **pang** in my rib cage."

Write a sentence using **pang**.

_____

_____

3 A third meaning of **stitch** includes the following related words.

a. **Half-cross** can mean a <u>type of loop or knot made in fabric</u>. For example, "My mother made my winter scarf with a fancy **half-cross**."

Write a sentence using **half cross**.

_____

_____

b. **Herringbone** can mean a <u>type of loop or knot made in fabric</u>. For example, "The old quilt on the bed was made by my great-gandmother using a **herringbone** design."

Write a sentence using **herringbone**.

_____

_____

c. **Cross-stitch** can mean a <u>type of loop or knot made in fabric</u>. For example, "My grandmother taught me how to **cross-stitch** when I was very young."

Write a sentence using **cross-stitch**.

_____

_____

Word Meaning in Context

Stitch began in the Old English language as a word meaning "a prick or puncture." Later, the meanings changed and expanded to include three current meanings:

- ❑ **tie together with staples or thread**
- ❑ **sudden sharp pain in the abdomen**
- ❑ **type of loop or knot made in fabric**

1. My Aunt Beverly tries to teach me how to make a different type of **stitch** for crocheting every time I visit her.

Which of the meanings of **stitch** is this? _____

_____

2. The doctor had to **stitch** up the wound to keep it from scarring.

Which of the meanings of **stitch** is this? _____

_____

3. I laughed so hard during the movie that I got a **stitch** in my side.

Which of the meanings of **stitch** is this? _____

_____

Word Meaning Map   The teacher will give you the **Stitch** worksheet.

Complete Each Definition

1. **Stitch** can mean a spasm or sudden sharp _____ in the abdomen.

2. **Stitch** can also mean a half-cross or type of loop or _____ made in fabric.

3. **Stitch** can also mean to sew or _____ together with staples or thread.

Understanding Check

Circle whether **stitch** is used as you would expect.

1. Jenny cut herself when she fell off the skateboard. The cut was deep enough that she had to go to the emergency room to have a doctor **stitch** it up.

   Expect   Not Expect

2. The nurse was getting the patient ready for surgery. The doctor would need to make a six-inch **stitch** in the patient before he could operate.

   Expect   Not Expect

3. My mother took me shopping for a new quilt. We bought one with the nicest colors and prettiest type of **stitch**.

   Expect   Not Expect

4. We did a mile run during P. E. class today. After I finished the race, I had a **stitch** in my side.

   Expect   Not Expect

5. My parents love to get massages. They say it is very relaxing, and it gives them a **stitch** in their muscles.

   Expect   Not Expect

6. My sister is going to paint her bedroom this weekend. She is looking for a **stitch** that both she and my parents will like.

   Expect   Not Expect

Create Stories

On a sheet of paper, write a short story or scenario for each of the three meanings of **stitch**.

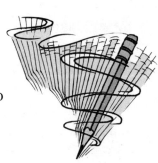

 **Tip**

Pre-Lesson Activity—Meanings of Related Words

1 One meaning of **tip** includes the following related words.

   a. **Top** can mean <u>pointed end of something</u>. For example, "On the **top** of the Sears Tower skyscraper is an observation deck where people can look out over the city of Chicago."
Write a sentence using **top**.

_____

_____

   b. **Peak** can mean <u>pointed end of something</u>. For example, "We couldn't see the **peak** of the mountain because of the clouds."
Write a sentence using **peak**.

_____

_____

   c. **Summit** can mean <u>pointed end of something</u>. For example, "The **summit** of Mount Everest reaches 29,035 feet."
Write a sentence using **summit**.

_____

_____

2 A second meaning of **tip** includes the following related words.

   a. **Reward** can mean <u>extra money given to someone for performing a service</u>. For example, "The young boy was hoping for a **reward** for doing a great job of washing the car."
Write a sentence using **reward**.

_____

_____

   b. **Gratuity** can mean <u>extra money given to someone for performing a service</u>. For example, "The menu at the restaurant said a **gratuity** would automatically be added to every bill."
Write a sentence using **gratutity**.

_____

_____

c. **Little something** can mean <u>extra money given to someone for performing a service</u>. For example, "My dad gave the taxi driver a **little something** for getting us to the airport quickly."

Write a sentence using **little something**.

_____

_____

3 A third meaning of **tip** includes the following related words.

a. **Hint** can mean a <u>useful piece of information</u>. For example, "The witness gave the police a **hint** about who committed the crime."

Write a sentence using **hint**.

_____

_____

b. **Recommendation** can mean a <u>useful piece of information</u>. For example, "The librarian gave me a **recommendation** about how to do my research report."

Write a sentence using **recommendation**.

_____

_____

c. **Suggestion** can mean a <u>useful piece of information</u>. For example, "The baseball coach gave the player a **suggestion** about how to improve his batting stance."

Write a sentence using **suggestion**.

_____

_____

4 A fourth meaning of **tip** includes the following related words.

a. **Tilt** can mean <u>cause to lean</u>. For example, "One of the couch legs is broken, so anyone who sits on it will **tilt** to the left."

Write a sentence using **tilt**.

_____

_____

b. **Slant** can mean <u>cause to lean</u>. For example, "A lot of rap musicians like to **slant** their baseball caps as a fashion statement."

Write a sentence using **slant**.

_____

_____

Word Meaning in Context

Tip began in the Old German language as a word meaning "light sharp blow or tap." Later, in the English language, the meanings changed and expanded to include four current meanings:

- ❑ **pointed end of something**
- ❑ **extra money given to someone for performing a service**
- ❑ **useful piece of information**
- ❑ **cause to lean**

1. The dog's wagging tail caused the vase to **tip** over.

Which of the meanings of **tip** is this? _____

_____

2. The **tip** of the pool cue broke off after I dropped it.

Which of the meanings of **tip** is this? _____

_____

3. The waiter was hoping for a big **tip** from the couple that came in all dressed up.

Which of the meanings of **tip** is this? _____

_____

4. My father said he got a **tip** about which horse will win the Kentucky Derby.

Which of the meanings of **tip** is this? _____

_____

Word Meaning Map   The teacher will give you the **Tip** worksheet.

Complete Each Definition

1. **Tip** can mean the top or _____ end of something.

2. **Tip** can also mean an extra reward or _____
given to someone for performing a service.

3. **Tip** can also mean a hint or useful piece of _____.

4. **Tip** can also mean to tilt or cause to _____.

Understanding Check

Circle whether **tip** is used as you would expect.

1. The term "**tip** of the iceberg" comes from science. Researchers claim that $\frac{7}{8}$ of an iceberg's mass is actually below water.   Expect   Not Expect

2. Kelly likes to talk about things nobody seems to care about. Even this morning, he gave me a **tip** that I couldn't care less about.   Expect   Not Expect

3. I made a vase in pottery class, but I didn't make the bottom flat. This causes the vase to **tip** over.   Expect   Not Expect

4. I accidentally hurt myself bowling last night. I dropped a ball on my foot when I tried to pick it up by its **tip**.   Expect   Not Expect

5. My family went out for dinner last night at an Italian restaurant. At the end of the meal, the waiter brought the **tip** to my parents.   Expect   Not Expect

6. My uncle always bets on the horses. He is always looking for a **tip** about which horse is favored to win.   Expect   Not Expect

7. Architects are people who make plans to build things. When constructing a tall skyscraper, they need to make sure the building will be safe and **tip** properly.   Expect   Not Expect

8. The bellhop at the hotel carried the luggage to our room. Afterward, my mother gave him several dollars as a **tip**.   Expect   Not Expect

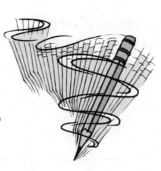

Create Stories

On a sheet of paper, write a short story or scenario for each of the four meanings of **tip**.

Pre-Lesson Activity—Meanings of Related Words

1 One meaning of **title** includes the following related words.

   a. **Heading** can mean a <u>name of a book, film, or other work</u>. For example, "The **heading** for my science paper was *The History of Dinosaurs*."
   Write a sentence using **heading**.

   _____

   _____

   b. **Caption** can mean a <u>name of a book, film, or other work</u>. For example, "The **caption** of the magazine article made me think it was about secret agents."
   Write a sentence using **caption**.

   _____

   _____

   c. **Credit** can mean a <u>name of a book, film, or other work</u>. For example, "I really liked the soundtrack for the movie and watched to see the **credit** for each of the songs played."
   Write a sentence using **credit**.

   _____

   _____

2 A second meaning of **title** includes the following related words.

   a. **Right** can mean a <u>legal document showing ownership</u>. For example, "The neighbors complained to my dad because they didn't believe he had the **right** to the land he was building a fence on."
   Write a sentence using **right**.

   _____

   _____

   b. **Claim** can mean a <u>legal document showing ownership</u>. For example, "In 1862, the Holmstead Act gave a **claim** of property in the Midwest to settlers who agreed to build a house and farm the land for five years."
   Write a sentence using **claim**.

   _____

   _____

c. **Bill of sale** can mean a <u>legal document showing ownership</u>. For example, "The trail boss had a **bill of sale** for all of the cattle he was driving."
Write a sentence using **bill of sale**.

_____

_____

3 A third meaning of **title** includes the following related words.

a. **Contest** can mean a <u>championship</u>. For example, "Every year at the state fair, my brother tries to win the pie-eating **contest**." Write a sentence using **contest**.

_____

_____

b. **Finals** can mean a <u>championship</u>. For example, "My sister's goal is to win the school's math **finals** this year." Write a sentence using **finals**.

_____

_____

c. **Competition** can mean a <u>championship</u>. For example, "I just watched Jeff Gordon win the stock-car racing **competition**." Write a sentence using **competition**.

_____

_____

4 A fourth meaning of **title** includes the following related words.

a. **Rank** means an <u>official position</u>. For example, "My brother is in the Marine Corps and holds the **rank** of captain."
Write a sentence using **rank**.

_____

_____

b. **Designation** can mean an <u>official position</u>. For example, "Since I oversee the construction crew, I have the **designation** of 'foreman.'"
Write a sentence using **designation**.

_____

_____

c. **Grade** can mean an <u>official position</u>. For example, "My dad is a very experienced builder, and holds the **grade** of Master Electrician."
Write a sentence using **grade**.

_____

_____

Word Meaning in Context

Title began in the Old French language as a word meaning "inscription or heading." Later, in the English language, the meanings expanded to include four current meanings:

- ❑ **name of a book, film, or other work**
- ❑ **legal document showing ownership**
- ❑ **championship**
- ❑ **official position**

1. I always call my physician by her **title** of Doctor.

Which of the meanings of **title** is this? _____

_____

2. I thought the movie might have English captions because the **title** was in Spanish.

Which of the meanings of **title** is this? _____

_____

3. My dad needed the **title** of the car to register it and get a new license plate.

Which of the meanings of **title** is this? _____

_____

4. The U.S. Open tennis championship is held each year in New York City to award the **title** to the best tennis players in the world.

Which of the meanings of **title** is this? _____

_____

Word Meaning Map   The teacher will give you the **Title** worksheet.

Complete Each Definition

1. **Title** can mean a heading or _____ of a book, film, or other work.

2. **Title** can also mean a claim or legal document showing _____.

3. **Title** can also mean a contest or _____.

4. **Title** can also mean a rank or _____ position of someone.

![checkmark] **Understanding Check**

Circle whether **title** is used as you would expect.

1. Last year my uncle started teaching math at the university.
   In his classroom, his students call him by the **title** of professor.   Expect   Not Expect

2. The baseball team I play for hasn't won a game all season.
   I'm sure we'll be playing for the **title**.   Expect   Not Expect

3. My favorite golfer is Tiger Woods. I was watching him win the
   British Open **title** on TV yesterday.   Expect   Not Expect

4. My grandfather gave the family farm to my mother when he
   retired. She went to the lawyer today to pick up the **title**.   Expect   Not Expect

5. I really like to read scary stories. The **title** of the book I'm
   reading now is Stephen King, who writes a lot of
   spooky stories.   Expect   Not Expect

6. My family rents an apartment downtown. We pay a **title**
   every month to the landlord so we can live there.   Expect   Not Expect

7. I was surprised the movie was a comedy. I never would have
   guessed it would be funny, given its **title**.   Expect   Not Expect

8. My mom gave birth to a baby boy yesterday. My new brother's
   title is Bob.   Expect   Not Expect

Create Stories

On a sheet of paper, write a short story or scenario
for each of the four meanings of **title**.

Toast

Pre-Lesson Activity—Meanings of Related Words

1 One meaning of **toast** includes the following related words.

a. **Pledge** can mean an <u>honor given to a person or event before drinking</u>. For example, "On Memorial Day, many Americans give a **pledge** to the soldiers that died in combat."

Write a sentence using **pledge**.

_____

_____

b. **Salute** can mean an <u>honor given to a person or event before drinking</u>. For example, "The race car driver gave a **salute** to his maintenance crew for helping him win the race."

Write a sentence using **salute**.

_____

_____

c. **Tribute** can mean an <u>honor given to a person or event before drinking</u>. For example, "The principal gave a **tribute** to the retiring science teacher in the lunchroom today."

Write a sentence using **tribute**.

_____

_____

2 A second meaning of **toast** includes the following related words.

a. **Warm up** can mean <u>heat up</u>. For example, "After walking to school in the cold rain, I just wanted to stand near the radiator and **warm up** my body."

Write a sentence using **warm up**.

_____

_____

b. **Thaw out** can mean <u>heat up</u>. For example, "Kyle said he needed to **thaw out** his hands after shoveling snow all afternoon."

Write a sentence using **thaw out**.

_____

_____

c. **Burn up** can mean <u>heat up</u>. For example, "Playing basketball outside in the hot sun made my body **burn up**."

Write a sentence using **burn up**.

_____

_____

3 A third meaning of **toast** has no related words.

a. When **toast** is used in this way, it means <u>sliced bread browned by heat</u>. For example, "I asked the waitress for more **toast**, since mine was burnt."

Write a sentence using **toast**.

_____

_____

Word Meaning in Context

Toast began in the Old French language as a word meaning "to brown or grill." Later, in the English language, the meanings expanded to include three current meanings:

❑ **honor given to a person or event before drinking**

❑ **heat up**

❑ **sliced bread browned by heat**

1. The waitress asked me if I wanted white or wheat **toast** with my breakfast.

Which of the meanings of **toast** is this? _____

_____

2. The best man at the wedding made a **toast** to the couple that was getting married.

Which of the meanings of **toast** is this? _____

_____

3. After skiing all morning in the cold, I sat by the heater to **toast** my hands.

Which of the meanings of **toast** is this? _____

_____

Word Meaning Map   The teacher will give you the **Toast** worksheet.

Complete Each Definition

1. **Toast** can mean a tribute or honor given to a person or event before

_____ .

2. **Toast** can also mean to warm up or _____ up.

3. **Toast** can also mean sliced _____ browned by heat.

Understanding Check

Circle whether **toast** is used as you would expect.

1. The story of *The Three Musketeers* is actually about four men who protect the king of France during the 17th century. These soldiers are called musketeers, and they often drink a **toast** to the king they protect.

   Expect   Not Expect

2. I really like to eat soft-boiled eggs. The best part is soaking up the yolk with a piece of **toast**.

   Expect   Not Expect

3. My dad was very upset with me for staying out too late last night, and he grounded me in front of my friends. I could not believe he would give me a **toast** in front of everyone like that.

   Expect   Not Expect

4. We had been four-wheeling in the hot desert for hours. I was afraid the extreme temperature would **toast** the engine.

   Expect   Not Expect

5. Whenever I visit my grandmother, we bake a different type of cake. The best part is trying a piece of **toast** after we bake it.

   Expect   Not Expect

6. The sodas we bought for the party were not cold enough to serve yet. My sister told us to leave them outside in the snow for a while to **toast** them.

   Expect   Not Expect

Create Stories

On a sheet of paper, write a short story or scenario for each of the three meanings of **toast**.

Trace

Pre-Lesson Activity—Meanings of Related Words

1 One meaning of **trace** includes the following related words.

    a. **Little bit** can mean a <u>very small amount of something</u>. For example, "The waiter at the Indian restaurant said that most of the meals had at least a **little bit** of curry in them."

       Write a sentence using **little bit**.

       _____

       _____

    b. **Scrap** can mean a <u>very small amount of something</u>. For example, "Five minutes after we fed leftovers to the dog, there wasn't a **scrap** of food in his bowl."

       Write a sentence using **scrap**.

       _____

       _____

    c. **Particle** can mean a <u>very small amount of something</u>. For example, "After the housekeeper cleaned, you couldn't find a **particle** of dirt in the room."

       Write a sentence using **particle**.

       _____

       _____

2 A second meaning of **trace** includes the following related words.

    a. **Find** can mean to <u>hunt down something</u>. For example, "The archaeologist was digging, trying to **find** evidence that early Native Americans had lived in the area."

       Write a sentence using **find**.

       _____

       _____

b. **Locate** can mean to <u>hunt down something</u>. For example, "The police were trying to **locate** the burglar who broke into the house."

Write a sentence using **locate**.

_____

_____

c. **Track** can mean to <u>hunt down something</u>. For example, "The Park Rangers tried to **track** the lost boy in the forest."

Write a sentence using **track**.

_____

_____

3 A third meaning of **trace** includes the following related words.

a. **Outline** can mean to <u>copy something</u>. For example, "Kerry is in kindergarten now, and she is learning how to **outline** letters of the alphabet."

Write a sentence using **outline**.

_____

_____

b. **Sketch** can mean to <u>copy something</u>. For example, "Travis likes to **sketch** pictures of different types of airplanes."

Write a sentence using **sketch**.

_____

_____

Word Meaning in Context

Trace began in the Latin language as a word meaning "be significant in."
Later, in the English language, this meaning changed and expanded
to include three current meanings:

- ❏ **very small amount of something**
- ❏ **hunt down something**
- ❏ **copy something**

1. The art teacher had the class **trace** a picture of a flower and then color it in.

Which of the meanings of **trace** is this? _____

_____

2. Sally said she could taste a **trace** of cherry flavor in her soda.

Which of the meanings of **trace** is this? _____

_____

3. The detectives were trying to **trace** the criminal who stole the car.

Which of the meanings of **trace** is this? _____

_____

Word Meaning Map   The teacher will give you the **Trace** worksheet.

Complete Each Definition

1. **Trace** can mean a particle or very _____
amount of something.

2. **Trace** can also mean evidence or _____ the existence
or presence of something.

3. **Trace** can also mean to outline, _____, or follow something.

Understanding Check

Circle whether **trace** is used as you would expect.

1. The recipe called for an entire bottle of vanilla flavoring. The chef added the **trace** of flavoring into the cake mix.

   Expect   Not Expect

2. Shawn is allergic to peanuts. He has to make sure there isn't a **trace** of peanuts in anything he eats.

   Expect   Not Expect

3. The little boy was making a Mother's Day card in kindergarten. He was trying to **trace** a picture of a heart for the front of the card.

   Expect   Not Expect

4. Daniel didn't like pickles. He had his mom **trace** some pickles at the market so he could eat them on his sandwich.

   Expect   Not Expect

5. The Park Rangers were trying to **trace** a mountain lion recently seen in the area. They were having trouble because heavy rains had washed away the animal's tracks.

   Expect   Not Expect

6. The professional artist was drawing funny sketches of people at the amusement park. Each picture was different, so the artist needed to **trace** every different person who paid him.

   Expect   Not Expect

Create Stories

On a sheet of paper, write a short story or scenario for each of the three meanings of **trace**.

| # Vision

Pre-Lesson Activity—Meanings of Related Words

1 One meaning of **vision** includes the following related words.

   a. **Eyeful** can mean a <u>beautiful person or thing</u>. For example, "To race car fans, the Ferrari F2001 Formula 1 is an **eyeful**."

   Write a sentence using **eyeful**.

   _____

   _____

   b. **Stunner** can mean a <u>beautiful person or thing</u>. For example, "All of Kyle's friends think his older sister Chantel is a **stunner**."

   Write a sentence using **stunner**.

   _____

   _____

   c. **Sight to behold** can mean a <u>beautiful person or thing</u>. For example, "Art critics claim Michelangelo's paintings on the ceiling of the Sistine chapel are a **sight to behold**."

   Write a sentence using **sight to behold**.

   _____

   _____

2 A second meaning of **vision** includes the following related words.

   a. **Dream** can mean an <u>image produced by the imagination</u>. For example, "Martin Luther King, Jr. gave a famous speech in which he said he had a **dream** that his children would live in a nation where they would not be judged by the color of their skin but by the content of their character."

   Write a sentence using **dream**.

   _____

   _____

b. **Foresight** can mean an <u>image produced by the imagination</u>. For example, "The founding fathers of this nation had the **foresight** to create this country as a democracy."

Write a sentence using **foresight**.

_____

_____

c. **Idea** can mean an <u>image produced by the imagination</u>. For example, "Henry Ford had an **idea** that it would be more productive to make cars using an assembly line."

Write a sentence using **idea**.

_____

_____

3 A third meaning of **vision** has no related words.

a. When **vision** is used in this way, it means <u>eyesight</u>. For example, "The nurse tested each student's **vision** in school yesterday."

Write a sentence using **vision**.

_____

_____

Word Meaning in Context

Vision began in the Latin language as a word meaning "sight or thing seen." Later, in the English language, the meanings expanded to include three current meanings:

- ❑ **beautiful person or thing**
- ❑ **image produced by the imagination**
- ❑ **eyesight**

1. Pilots are tested to make sure they have 20/20 **vision** for flying.

Which of the meanings of **vision** is this? _____

_____

2. Craig thought the first Harley-Davidson motorcycle he saw was a **vision**.

Which of the meanings of **vision** is this? _____

_____

3. Bill Gates had a **vision** that the demand for home computers would create the need for more software, so he created a company called Microsoft to make computer programs.

Which of the meanings of **vision** is this? _____

_____

Word Meaning Map   The teacher will give you the **Vision** worksheet.

Complete Each Definition

1. **Vision** can mean a _____ person or thing.

2. **Vision** can also mean the ability to _____.

3. **Vision** can also mean a dream or image produced by the _____.

Understanding Check

Circle whether **vision** is used as you would expect.

1. Joan of Arc was a young girl who had a **vision** that she could save France from an English invasion during the 15th century. She successfully led an army that drove the English from the French town of Orleans.

   Expect   Not Expect

2. Lyle's room is always a mess, with clothes thrown everywhere. His mother is usually upset with him because his room is such a **vision**.

   Expect   Not Expect

3. Brent was applying for his drivers permit at the Department of Motor Vehicles. Before they would give him a permit, they made him read from an eye chart to check his **vision**.

   Expect   Not Expect

4. The Eiffel tower was built in Paris for the World Expo in 1889. The 300-meter tower was the largest in the world and was called a **vision** by those who saw it for the first time.

   Expect   Not Expect

5. The doctor hit the patient's knee with a small instrument under his kneecap during his exam. The patient's leg kicked, so the doctor thought his **vision** was okay.

   Expect   Not Expect

6. Kramer did not know the answer to the final question on his test. After a few minutes, he just put his pen down and gave up, since his mind was a **vision**.

   Expect   Not Expect

Create Stories

On a sheet of paper, write a short story or scenario for each of the three meanings of **vision**.

The Multiple Meaning Vocabulary Program

Waste

Pre-Lesson Activity—Meanings of Related Words

1 One meaning of **waste** includes the following related words.

   a. **Junk** can mean discarded materials or <u>garbage</u>. For example, "People often throw their unwanted and broken appliances away because they consider them to be **junk**."

     Write a sentence using **junk**.

     _____

     _____

   b. **Trash** can mean <u>garbage</u>. For example, "We consider wrappers, old cans, and used cups to be **trash**."

     Write a sentence using **trash**.

     _____

     _____

   c. **Rubbish** can mean worthless items or <u>garbage</u>. For example, "While walking through the alley, Adam saw a puppy poke its head out of a pile of **rubbish**."

     Write a sentence using **rubbish**.

     _____

     _____

2 A second meaning of **waste** includes the following related words.

   a. **Blow** can mean to spend too much or <u>throw away or misuse</u>. For example, "Daisy's grandma told her to save her birthday money for a rainy day and not **blow** it."

     Write a sentence using **blow**.

     _____

     _____

b. **Ruin** can mean to destroy or <u>throw away or misuse</u>. For example, "Duncan decided to go to the fair and check out the horse races. Duncan's mother warned him not to **ruin** his good shoes by wearing them in the mud."

Write a sentence using **ruin**.

_____

_____

c. **Squander** can mean to <u>throw away or misuse</u>. For example, "Maria's father put her money into a college trust fund so that Maria would not **squander** it."

Write a sentence using **squander**.

_____

_____

3 A third meaning of **waste** includes the following related words.

a. **Corrode** can mean to <u>dwindle or become slowly weaker</u>. For example, "The statue's face began to **corrode** away over the years due to being exposed to the weather."

Write a sentence using **corrode**.

_____

_____

b. **Spoil** can mean to <u>dwindle or become slowly weaker</u>. For example, "The produce from the store must have been old, because after four days the fruit began to **spoil**."

Write a sentence using **spoil**.

_____

_____

c. **Wither** can mean to <u>dwindle or become slowly weaker</u>. For example, "Mrs. James got flowers, but after a couple of days the flowers began to **wither** away."

Write a sentence using **wither**.

_____

_____

Word Meaning in Context

Waste began in the Old North French language as a word meaning "make empty." Later, in the English language, this meaning changed and expanded to include three current meanings:

- ❑ **garbage**
- ❑ **throw away or misuse**
- ❑ **dwindle or become slowly weaker**

1. For a community service project, I began picking up **waste** along the side of the highway.

Which of the meanings of **waste** is this? _____

_____

2. Josh bought apples and forgot to eat them, so they went to **waste**.

Which of the meanings of **waste** is this? _____

_____

3. The old dog was not eating and began to **waste** away.

Which of the meanings of **waste** is this? _____

_____

Word Meaning Map   The teacher will give you the **Waste** worksheet.

Complete Each Definition

1. **Waste** can mean rubbish or _____.

2. **Waste** can also mean to throw away or _____.

3. **Waste** can also mean to dwindle or become slowly _____.

Understanding Check

Circle whether **waste** is used as you would expect.

1. Casey needed to clean his room. His mother demanded that he take his **waste** out because it was overflowing from the can.

    Expect   Not Expect

2. Jennifer's mother bought her oranges because they are her favorite. Before Jennifer went to bed, she let her orange go to **waste** because she ate it.

    Expect   Not Expect

3. Jasper started taking his vitamins and eating healthier. After a month he could run faster because his good eating habits made him **waste** away.

    Expect   Not Expect

4. As Andrea was getting ready for the school dance, she put on a little bit of her mother's perfume. She didn't want to **waste** any because it was so expensive.

    Expect   Not Expect

5. Tiffany's grandmother gave her a diamond ring for her 18th birthday. Tiffany put the ring in a pile of **waste** because she wanted to keep it clean and safe.

    Expect   Not Expect

6. As the water washed over the stone for thousands of years, the stone began to break down and **waste** away. It was smaller and misshapen because of this erosion.

    Expect   Not Expect

Create Stories

On a sheet of paper, write a short story or scenario for each of the three meanings of **waste**.

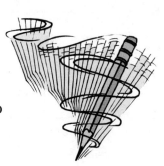

 Pre-Lesson Activity—Meanings of Related Words

1   One meaning of **well** includes the following related words.

  a. **Repository** can mean a <u>source of water, oil, or gas in the ground</u>. For example, "The oil tycoon was excited to find that he had more oil in his underground **repository** than he expected."

  Write a sentence using **repository**.

  _____

  _____

  b. **Reservoir** can mean a <u>source of water, oil, or gas in the ground</u>. For example, "Banks Lake was created from the Columbia River; this **reservoir** supplies water to almost all of the crops in the basin area of Washington."

  Write a sentence using **reservoir**.

  _____

  _____

  c. **Spring** can mean a <u>source of water, oil, or gas in the ground</u>. For example, "Jamie's grandma did not want people spraying chemicals because she was worried about the effect they would have on the **spring**."

  Write a sentence using **spring**.

  _____

  _____

2   A second meaning of **well** includes the following related words.

  a. **Fountain** can mean a <u>source of something</u>. For example, "Jonathan was a **fountain** of knowledge; whenever we had a question, we would go ask him."

  Write a sentence using **fountain**.

  _____

  _____

b. **Origin** can mean the point at which something comes into existence or a <u>source of something</u>. For example, "Sarah did not know the **origin** of the chain letter."

Write a sentence using **origin**.

_____

_____

c. **Root** can mean a <u>source of something</u>. For example, "Many people believe that the **root** of all evil begins with money or power."

Write a sentence using **root**.

_____

_____

3 A third meaning of **well** includes the following related words.

a. **Successfully** can mean <u>good or right</u>. For example, "Dirk's mother always told her friends about how her son was doing so **successfully** in his job."

Write a sentence using **successfully**.

_____

_____

b. **Properly** can mean <u>good or right</u>. For example, "Diana's boss told her that she was doing her job **properly**."

Write a sentence using **properly**.

_____

_____

c. **Splendidly** can mean <u>good or right</u>. For example, "Jason's grandma always talks about how **splendidly** her grandson is doing in college."

Write a sentence using **splendidly**.

_____

_____

Word Meaning in Context

Well began in the French language as a word meaning "healthy party." Later, in the English language, this meaning expanded to include three current meanings:

- ❏ **source of water, oil, or gas in the ground**
- ❏ **source of something**
- ❏ **good or right**

1. Bree was doing **well** in school and was on the honor roll all year long.

Which of the meanings of **well** is this?_____

_____

2. Mrs. Anthony was worried that the chemicals from the crop spraying would get into her **well**.

Which of the meanings of **well** is this?_____

_____

3. Mr. Ayers was a **well** of knowledge when it came to science and math.

Which of the meanings of **well** is this?_____

_____

Word Meaning Map   The teacher will give you the **Well** worksheet.

Complete Each Definition

1. **Well** can mean a source of _____,
oil, or gas in the ground.

2. **Well** can also mean _____ or origin.

3. **Well** can also mean _____ or right.

Understanding Check

Circle whether **well** is used as you would expect.

1. James failed his last spelling test. His teacher told him he was doing very **well** in spelling.

   Expect   Not Expect

2. Christina's dad went outside to check the level of the **well**. Water wasn't coming out of the faucets in their home.

   Expect   Not Expect

3. Abby's grandmother was such a **well** of knowledge when it came to cooking. Everyone asked her for special recipes.

   Expect   Not Expect

4. Jessica's family stopped on the bridge to take pictures. The **well** was beautiful, flowing down the mountain and into the valley.

   Expect   Not Expect

5. Jackson's mother always bragged to her book club about how **well** her son was doing on the college basketball team and in school. Everyone loved hearing about Jackson.

   Expect   Not Expect

6. Jimmy did not know anything about landscaping his yard. His neighbors considered him to be a **well** of knowledge about plants, trees, flowers, and other landscaping needs.

   Expect   Not Expect

Create Stories

On a sheet of paper, write a short story or scenario for each of the three meanings of **well**.

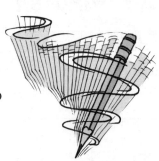

Worry

Pre-Lesson Activity—Meanings of Related Words

1 One meaning of **worry** includes the following related words.

    a. **Despair** can mean <u>emotional upset</u>. For example, "Jackie didn't mean to cause John **despair**, but she thought he should know that his grandmother was sick."

       Write a sentence using **despair**.

       _____

       _____

    b. **Torment** can mean <u>emotional upset</u>. For example, "The memory of the fight with his brother caused James much **torment**."

       Write a sentence using **torment**.

       _____

       _____

    c. **Distress** can mean <u>emotional upset</u>. For example, "The tornado caused much **distress** to the people who lost their homes in the destruction."

       Write a sentence using **distress**.

       _____

       _____

2 A second meaning of **worry** has no related words.

    a. When **worry** is used in this way, it means to <u>grab with the teeth and shake</u>. For example, "Bradley's mother told him not to let the dog outside because it would **worry** the cat and hurt it."

       Write a sentence using **worry**.

       _____

       _____

3 A third meaning of **worry** includes the following related words.

a. **Alarm** can mean to <u>make upset</u>. For example, "I didn't mean to **alarm** my mom when I told her I was staying out late tonight."

Write a sentence using **alarm**.

_____

_____

b. **Unsettle** can mean to disrupt or <u>make upset</u>. For example, "Derek knew that his father and mother hadn't meant to **unsettle** him with their fighting, but he was nervous just the same."

Write a sentence using **unsettle**.

_____

_____

c. **Disconcert** can mean to <u>make upset</u>. For example, "You had better tell your mother that you are going to spend the night because you wouldn't want to **disconcert** her."

Write a sentence using **disconcert**.

_____

_____

Word Meaning in Context

Worry began in the Old English language as a word meaning "to strangle." Later, this meaning changed and expanded to include three current meanings:

- ❑ **emotional upset**
- ❑ **grab with the teeth and shake**
- ❑ **make upset**

1. Dawn was told that she shouldn't **worry** about her mother because it was just a simple operation.

Which of the meanings of **worry** is this? _____

_____

2. Steven has a **worry** that he will fail his math test because he does not know how to answer a lot of the problems.

Which of the meanings of **worry** is this? _____

_____

3. Jack's father took the snake away from the dog because the dog was going to **worry** it to death.

Which of the meanings of **worry** is this? _____

_____

Word Meaning Map   The teacher will give you the **Worry** worksheet.

Complete Each Definition

1. **Worry** can mean _____ upset or distress.

2. **Worry** can also mean to grab with the _____ and shake.

3. **Worry** can also mean to make _____ .

Understanding Check

Circle whether **worry** is used as you would expect.

1. The puppy grabbed the scarf off of my neck. He ran to the yard and began to **worry** it.　　　　Expect　　　Not Expect

2. Jasmine always walks around with a big smile on her face. She acts as if she doesn't have a **worry** on her mind.　　　　Expect　　　Not Expect

3. Dorina needed help on her project, so Ms. Jameson said she could help her after school. Ms. Jameson reminded Dorina to call her mother so she wouldn't **worry** about her coming home late.　　　　Expect　　　Not Expect

4. Chris didn't have a **worry** about anything. He was so stressed that he began to cry when he forgot his homework.　　　　Expect　　　Not Expect

5. Shane never touched the knot on the rope. His brother came home and was happy that he had left the rope alone, taking the time to **worry** it.　　　　Expect　　　Not Expect

6. Missy was happy all weekend. She said she began to **worry** about everything as she sat in the sun and relaxed. She had a great weekend.　　　　Expect　　　Not Expect

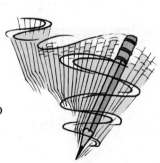

Create Stories

On a sheet of paper, write a short story or scenario for each of the three meanings of **worry**.

Young

Pre-Lesson Activity—Meanings of Related Words

1 One meaning of **young** includes the following related words.

a. **Kids** can mean <u>children</u> who are no longer babies. For example, "The **kids** seem to enjoy the snow more than the adults do."

Write a sentence using **kids**.

_____

_____

b. **Juveniles** can mean <u>children</u> or someone who is not yet an adult. For example, "Ricky observed that the **juveniles** had more energy than the adults did during the annual father/son basketball game."

Write a sentence using **juveniles**.

_____

_____

c. **Youths** can mean <u>children</u> and young persons as a group. For example, "Those who were **youths** received a free book from the local bookstore during a campaign to promote reading in the community."

Write a sentence using **youths**.

_____

_____

2 A second meaning of **young** includes the following related words.

a. **Offspring** can mean the <u>babies of an animal</u>. For example, "Cierra enjoyed living on a farm and being able to watch animals care for their **offspring**."

Write a sentence using **offspring**.

_____

_____

b. **Litter** can mean the <u>babies of an animal</u> born to one mother on a single occasion. For example, "Darren had his pick of the **litter** when he went to get a new puppy at his uncle's ranch."

Write a sentence using **litter**.

_____

_____

c. **Progeny** can mean the <u>babies of an animal</u>. For example, "Linda liked caring for the **progeny** of the old mother cat."

Write a sentence using **progeny**.

_____

_____

3 A third meaning of **young** includes the following related words.

a. **Inexperienced** can mean that someone is in the <u>early stage of life, growth, or development</u> and has a lack of knowledge and experience. For example, "The students are **inexperienced** musicans who need a lot of instruction and practice."

Write a sentence using **inexperienced**.

_____

_____

b. **Childish** can mean that someone's behavior is typical of a person who is in the <u>early stage of life, growth, or development</u>. For example, "The teacher was surprised that the students displayed such **childish** manners in the lunchroom."

Write a sentence using **childish**.

_____

_____

c. **Immature** can mean that someone is in the <u>early stage of life, growth, or development</u> and not yet completely grown. For example, "The bear was still **immature** and did not have babies yet."

Write a sentence using **immature**.

_____

_____

Word Meaning in Context

Young began in the Old Indo-European languages as a word meaning "youthful." Later, in the English language, this meaning expanded to include three current meanings:

- ❏ **children**
- ❏ **babies of an animal**
- ❏ **early stage of life, growth, or development**

1. Kaleb's father works as a salesperson for a **young** company.

Which of the meanings of **young** is this? _____

_____

2. Skateboarding is an activity primarily for the **young**.

Which of the meanings of **young** is this? _____

_____

3. Candice thought it was interesting to watch a mother hen protecting her **young**.

Which of the meanings of **young** is this? _____

_____

Word Meaning Map   The teacher will give you the **Young** worksheet.

Complete Each Definition

1. Young can mean kids or _____who are

no longer babies.

2. Young can also mean _____ of life, growth, or development.

3. Young can also mean _____ of an animal or a litter.

Understanding Check

Circle whether **young** is used as you would expect.

1. Rodney and his sister Naomi loved to spend time at the children's museum because it was designed with the **young** in mind. It had lots of fun things to see and do.

    Expect   Not Expect

2. For Grandparents Day, Teresa invited her grandparents to come to school. They were thrilled that a special day had been set aside to honor the **young** like themselves.

    Expect   Not Expect

3. When Meredith visited a forest in California, she learned that redwood trees regularly reach 600 years of age. She enjoyed seeing such **young** trees.

    Expect   Not Expect

4. When Mark and Mia went to the movie, they saw a sign that said that the **young** pay an admission charge, but children get in free.

    Expect   Not Expect

5. Ellen enjoyed spending time outside in her backyard. One day, Ellen saw a mother bird fly back to her nest to feed her **young**.

    Expect   Not Expect

6. Let's go to the zoo and see the tiger's **young**. I heard that they have four tigers that are several years old.

    Expect   Not Expect

Create Stories

On a sheet of paper, write a short story or scenario for each of the three meanings of **young**.